PLAYTIME DISHES

by
Lorraine May Punchard

Library of Congress # 76-58068
ISBN # 0-87069-212-7

Photography by
Gary Sherman

Published By

Wallace-Homestead Book Co.
1912 Grand Avenue
Des Moines, Iowa 50309

Cover photograph: German doll dishes circa 1900

Dedication

RICHARD VICTOR PUNCHARD
whose encouragement and
understanding made this
book possible.

Acknowledgments

*I wish to express my sincere thanks to
Irene E. Prochnow for sharing her knowledge of antiques
and for her encouragement while I was writing this book.
And a very special thank you to a dear friend for
lending items found in the color section. Her dolls,
teddy bears, ice cream table and chairs, dresser,
washstand and toilet set made the settings complete.
The sweet little girls who so willingly posed for
the settings are Melissa Krei and Mercedes Henderson.
Thank you, girls!*

"This is like being a little girl again," a friend said to me as we ↱t the child's table with the service from the small china ↱pboard. We had chosen "Humphrey's Clock" for the dinner ↱rvice and "Fernland" for the glassware.

I glanced at the "Kate Greenaway" dishes which took my ↱ind back over the years of collecting. During these years, I ↱ave not found a reference work devoted expressly to children's ↱laytime dishes. It is my desire that this book will aid others ↱aving the same interest.

I have, intentionally, tried not to include pieces found in ↱useums, but, rather, have focused upon the antique and ↱llectible dishes found in today's market. I have included ↱anufacturers' marks whenever possible; otherwise, the sets are ↱nmarked. The color of the mark is in parentheses.

Sets of children's play dishes were made in tea sets, coffee or ↱coa sets, and dinner service sets. Their size depended on the ↱tended use. The larger sets were meant to be used by little ↱rls, having parties for their friends and for practicing the social ↱aces of the times. The cups were approximately demitasse size. ↱he smaller sets were made for little girls to have parties with ↱eir dolls, or for their dolls to have parties among themselves; ↱erefore, the smaller sizes were often referred to as "doll ↱shes." However, there is still a smaller size, usually called ↱iniature dollhouse size.

According to the taste and means of the family, children's ↱aytime dishes were a smaller scale of the family china. ↱rading ranged from fair to exceptionally fine.

The United States imported large quantities of children's play ↱shes from Europe prior to the start of World War I in 1914. ↱pan became the chief exporter of children's play sets to the ↱nited States between the two World Wars, again after the ↱cond World War, and continues to be chief exporter today. ↱he United States is noted mainly for "Akro Agate" and ↱Depression Glass" manufactured during the 1930s and 1940s.

The first known porcelain came from China, and since that ↱me the word "china" is used as a handy overall word for ↱ttery and porcelain.

The measurements given in the descriptions are to the nearest ↱ inch, because in many cases the pieces will vary a little in the ↱me set.

I fully realize that there are many sets unknown to me at this ↱me; however, the intention of this book is to help collectors and ↱alers identify and attribute children's playtime dishes.

Any responses to this book may be addressed to me in care of ↱e publisher along with a self-addressed, stamped envelope. I ↱ll cheerfully try to answer your letter as soon as possible.

Tea Sets

Notice the quality and interesting shapes of the sets pictured. Some are of very fine quality and craftsmanship, while others were made with many flaws and, I'm sure, were intended to be used, played with, and ultimately broken. The finer sets would have been more of a teaching tool in Victorian times. This era reflects the styles and customs in the years from about 1840 to 1890 and, particularly, the Civil War period.

When referring to a tea set of six place settings, articles included usually consist of teapot and cover, sugar bowl and cover, creamer, six cups, six saucers, and six plates for a total of twenty-three pieces. A set of four place settings would have seventeen pieces. Sets with a waste bowl would have one additional piece. Are you thinking, what is a waste bowl? When you were served a second cup of tea, the remains in your cup were emptied into the waste bowl and you were given fresh tea. You never added to the tea in your cup.

Many of the doll-sized sets didn't have tea plates, but may have had a cookie serving plate with two small handles.

The character figures, (Kate Greenaway, Kewpies, etc.) were derived from articles, books, comic strips, toys, and dolls. Replicas of these characters were made into transfers to be put on children's play dishes.

To Make Tea

Have ready a kettle of water boiling fast, pour some into the teapot, let it remain for a few minutes, then throw it out; measure a teaspoonful of tea for each two persons, put it in the pot, pour on it about a gill of boiling water, cover it close for five minutes, then fill it up; have a covered pitcher of boiling water with it; when two cups are poured from it, fill it up; you will thus keep the strength good and equal. If the company is large, it is best to have some of the tea drawn in the covered pitcher, and replenish the tea-pot or urn when it is exhausted.

From *THE EVERYDAY COOKBOOK* (published circa 1880).

Kate Greenaway, a famous illustrator (1846-1901), created original dress designs of quaint, graceful, fascinating children. Her first book, *Under the Window* was published in England in 1878. Kate Greenaway wrote the verses and created the styles. She had a feeling for original designs, color, and landscape. This book had a startling effect in the reform of children's dress from the previous Victorian styles. The craze was to copy the slim Empire gowns, sashes, puffed sleeves with lace or ruffles, and sunbonnets of Kate Greenaway girls.

These designs were used on many items from England, France, Germany, America, and other countries. Many china and porcelain factories copied Kate Greenaway designs in their decorating.

Scenes of children out-of-doors. Manufactured in England circa 1880. Height of the teapot, 4½ inches. Diameter of a plate, 4¾ inches. Set of four with waste bowl.

11

KATE GREENAWAY
From the book *Under the Window*

Scenes of Brownies in action. German porcelain circa 1900. Teapot height, 4 ½ inches. Plate diameter, 3 ⅛ inches. Set of two (no creamer).

The twelve Miss Pelicoes
  Were twelve sweet little girls;
Some wore their hair in pigtail plaits,
  And some of them wore curls.

The twelve Miss Pelicoes
  Had dinner every day;—
A not uncommon thing at all,
  You probably will say.

The twelve Miss Pelicoes
  Went sometimes for a walk;
It also is a well-known fact
  That all of them could talk.

The twelve Miss Pelicoes
  Were always most polite,—
Said "If you please," and "Many thanks,
  "Good morning," and "Good night."

The twelve Miss Pelicoes,
  You plainly see, were taught
To do the things they didn't like,
  Which means, the things they ought.

Now, fare ye well, Miss Pelicoes,
  I wish ye a good day;—
About these twelve Miss Pelicoes
  I've nothing more to say.

The twelve Miss Pelicoes
  Of course, to school were sent;
Their parents wished them to excel
  In each accomplishment.

The twelve Miss Pelicoes
  Played music—*Fal-lal-la!*
Which consequently made them all
  The pride of their papa.

The twelve Miss Pelicoes
  Learnt dancing and the globes;
Which proves that they were wise, and had
  That patience which was Job's.

K.G

Brownies — Palmer Cox (1840-1924) created the version of these elfinlike creatures from the folklore legends of Scotland told to him by his Scottish grandmother.

Mr. Cox said "Brownies, like fairies, were imaginary little sprites who were supposed to delight in harmless pranks while weary households slept, and never allowed themselves to be seen by mortals." The first Brownie drawings and stories appeared in *St. Nicholas* magazine in 1883. *The Brownies, Their Book* was published in 1887. palmer Cox copyrighted and patented twelve Brownie figures in 1892, and these figures were used for many items. In 1895, the Brownie craze even extended into children's tea sets.

Rose Cecil O'Neill (1874-1944) was a naturally gifted person. She was a self-taught artist and the creator of the famous Kewpies, who first appeared in 1909. She said the Kewpies, elflike creatures, came to her in a dream. She loved children and brought out their characteristics in the Kewpies. The topknot was that little wisp of hair that stands up on the head after the baby has been asleep.

Children's play dishes, with the Kewpie decals, were made by Royal Rudolstadt in Prussia and companies in Germany, Bavaria and Czechoslovakia.

Signed — Germany circa 1915. Teapot height, 5½ inches. Saucer diameter, 4½ inches. Set of six — no plates.

Today wild sprigs of Mistletoe
On chandeliers will strangely grow
And here and there, where lights are dim
You'll spy Her being kissed by Him
And if a Kewp should catch you there
Beware, Fair Lady, Oh beware!

(red)

Happifats were designed from drawings by Kate Jordan. In 1914 Borgfeldt registered these figures as a trademark in the United States and Germany. They were popular at the time of the Kewpies.

Beyer & Bock porcelain manufacturers from Volkstedt-Rudolstadt, Germany made this Happifats coffee set.

Happifats in action and strawberries are depicted on all the pieces. The porcelain is white with a blue band on the rims. Included in this set are a coffeepot and cover, creamer, covered sugar, four plates, four cups and saucers.

Coffeepot height, 6 inches. Plate diameter, 5½ inches.

Here we are at the party.
Three little girls and three little dolls.
It is a Sunbonnet Babies' party.
See what good things we have to eat.
Don't you wish you had some?
We cannot give you any.
It is all for us.
This is our party.

Bertha L. Corbett Melcher was the creator of Molly and May, better known as the Sunbonnet Babies. She could show character and feeling without showing a face. The Sunbonnet

Babies were popular in a period extending from the 1890 int[o] the 1920s. The picture and verse were from *The Sunbonnet Babies Book* by Eulalie Osgood Grover, illustrated by Berth[a] Corbett Melcher, published in 1902.

Teapot height, 4½ inches including handle. Plate diameter, 4½ inches.

The scenes Sunday, fishing; Monday, washing; Tuesday, ironing; Wednesday, mending; Thursday, scrubbing; Friday, sweeping; and Saturday, baking; were applied on a set of seve[n] porcelain plates produced by Royal Bayreuth, Bavaria, Germany.

Children's tea sets have also been made with the Sunbonne[t] Babies' decor.

Buster Brown was created by Richard Felton Outcault (1863-
928). He began as a newspaper cartoonist and, in 1902, created
e characters, Buster Brown, his sister Mary Jane, and Tige the
ulldog. They were designed from the likenesses of his own
hildren and dog.

Buster Brown always had a prank to play, but the pranks were
ever mean, and the strip always concluded with a useful little
rmon for the children.

ampbell Kids..

The name "Campbell Kids" came from the Campbell Soup
ompany advertising which began in 1900.

Grace Gebbie (Weiderseim) Drayton (1877-1936) was the
reator of the Campbell Kids and drew them for approximately
fteen years for Campbell Soup.

An article, "The Campbell Kids and Their Times" was
ublished in the *Antique Journal,* January 1973, by Mildred
eley Hardcastle in which she said: "The Campbell Kids also
ppeared on ceramics made by the Buffalo Pottery." The
ecember 1973 issue of *Antique Journal* carried an article
ntitled, "The Multiple Talents of Grace Gebbie Drayton," in
hich Gladys Hollander said: "Daintier plates with lustre and
calloped edges also bore the likeness of the (Campbell)
hildren. These were the product of the D. E. McNichol
ompany of East Liverpool, Ohio. Plates, pin trays and other
hina pieces bore the likeness of the doll. Some of the pieces
ere in lovely Bavarian China."

Buster Brown, Mary Jane, and Tige on German
porcelain circa 1905. Teapot height, 5¼ inches. Plate
diameter, 5 inches. Set of four.

Alice in Wonderland, the children's classic, was written by
harles Lutwidge Dodgson, who used the pen name, Lewis
arroll. He loved children and in 1862, told a story to a little
irl, Alice Lidell, which he called "Alice's Adventures
nderground." In 1865 the story was published as *Alice in
onderland.*

The characters on the tea set are exact copies from the
riginal engravings by John Tenniel. This set recently came
rom England and the only mark is the Rd. 446135 which would

Teapot height, 3½ inches. Saucer diameter, 3¾ inches.

date the set, 1904. The porcelain is German and was probabl made as a special order for a company in England.

The characters on this set include the following:

Teapot and one cup—Humpty Dumpty extending a hand to Alice.

Creamer and one cup—Alice holding a flamingo, with the Duchess at her side.

Sugar—Alice at a tea party under a tree, with the Hatter, Marc Hare, and Dormouse.

One cup—The Duchess nursing a baby, the cook, a cheshire ca and Alice.

One cup—Alice, Tweedledum, and Tweedledee standing under tree.

The four saucers are a plain green.

R <u>d</u>
446 135   (red)

German porcelain circa 1910. Coffeepot height, 5½ inches. Plate diameter, 5¼ inches. Set of six.

The Santa Claus on these German dishes resembles a bishc more than he resembles the Santa Claus of today.

The Santa Claus as we know today has developed from th trends, customs, and beliefs of several countries.

St. Nicholas was a bishop in the fourth century and later became a patron saint. Legends which originally portrayed S Nicholas as a giver to the poor later depicted him as a giver c gifts to the children. The colors red and white were a symbol c the bishop's garb.

Christ-Kindlein is the German proper name for Christ-chilc This gradually became "Kris-Kringle." In England he was called Father Christmas and in France, Papa Noel. The Dutc Sinterklass gradually became Santa Claus.

The teddy bear was inspired by a story about Theodore Roosevelt after he refused to shoot a bear cub on a hunting tri This incident happened in 1902 and by 1904 the teddy bear was well known toy. Teddy bear designs were used on numerous items for decoration, including tea sets.

This plate was made in Germany with a pink luster bord that measures 5 inches in diameter.

Teapot height, 3 ¾ inches. Plate diameter, 3 ¾ inches.
Cake plate diameter, 4 ¼ inches.

(red) LICENSED BY
FAMOUS ARTISTS
SYNDICATE
MADE IN JAPAN

Little Orphan Annie was a comic strip character created by
Harold Gray (1894-1968).

Mr. Gray was working as a cartoonist for the *New York
Daily News* in 1924, when he started the comic strip, "Little
Orphan Annie."

The comic strip had suspense, romance, danger, and thrills in
it and became an indispensable part of daily papers across
America.

These Orphan Annie dishes with the caramel colored border
were made in Japan. Each plate has a different scene of Orphan
Annie and her dog, Sandy. This set consists of a teapot,
creamer, sugar, cake plate, and six place settings.

Walter Elias Disney (1901-1966), better known as Walt
Disney, was the producer of animated cartoons and the creator
of Mickey Mouse and Donald Duck. Mickey Mouse was
introduced in the first sound cartoon, *Steamboat Willie*,
produced in 1928.

Children's play dishes with the Disney characters were
generally made in Japan in the 1930s. These were made with
luster and were an inexpensive toy that was meant to be played
with. Toy tin dishes were also made with Disney characters
either painted on or impressed into the mold.

MICKEY MOUSE
CORP. by
WALT E. DISNEY
MADE IN JAPAN

Betty Boop was drawn as an animated cartoon, created by
Max Fleischer for Fleischer Studios circa 1932. Betty Boop
represents a movie queen of the 1930s. This design has been used
on play dishes.

17

It is always exciting to find English play dishes because the English were precise in their markings, thus making it easier to determine the manufacturer and the date.

Children's Staffordshire tea sets were made for the export trade, mainly from the early 1800s to the early 1900s. These sets usually have a white background and a design in one basic color of blue, brown, or red.

English sets often have a crazing (the small cracks on the surface glaze). This is one distinction that can help determine the sets' origins.

Staffordshire potteries are located in a district in midwestern England, southeast of Liverpool. Besides the large firms of Copeland, Minton, and Wedgwood, this area possessed hundreds of smaller factories in the main towns or districts of Burslem, Cobridge, Etruria, Fenton, Hanley, Lane End, Longton, Longport, Stoke, and Tunstall. In 1910, towns of this district merged to form the present city of Stoke-on-Trent. The smaller potteries mainly produced ordinary domestic earthenware for export trade.

English tea sets made during this time period included a waste bowl and are not considered complete without one. The sugar bowls in the same period were almost the size of the teapot. The sugar was coarse, not like the refined sugar of today.

These marks were registered in the British Patent Office. The diamond-shaped registration marks were used from 1842-1883. Two patterns were used during this time period. The parcel number identifies the manufacturer.

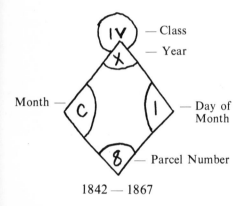

Month — Class / Year / Day of Month / Parcel Number

1842 — 1867

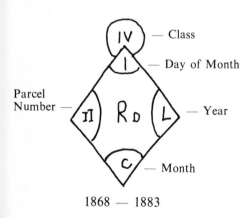

Parcel Number — Class / Day of Month / Year / Month

1868 — 1883

The code for the months is as follows:

January	— C or O	July	— I
February	— G	August	— R
March	— W	September	— D
April	— H	October	— B
May	— E	November	— K
June	— M	December	— A

the code for the year date is as follows:

1882-1867		1868-1883	
A — 1845	N — 1864	A — 1871	L — 1882
B — 1858	O — 1862	C — 1870	P — 1877
C — 1844	P — 1851	D — 1878	S — 1875
D — 1852	Q — 1866	E — 1881	U — 1874
E — 1855	R — 1861	F — 1873	V — 1876
F — 1847	S — 1849	H — 1869	W — 1878
G — 1863	T — 1867	I — 1872	X — 1868
H — 1843	U — 1848	J — 1880	Y — 1879
I — 1846	V — 1850	K — 1883	
J — 1854	W — 1865		
K — 1857	X — 1842		
L — 1856	Y — 1853		
M — 1859	Z — 1860		

the class number in the top circle designates the material.
I—Metal; II—Wood; III—Glass; IV—Earthenware

From 1884 design registration numbers were used. Rd. 1 was registered in January, 1884. The following numbers are for January first of each year.

Approximate Numbers

1884 —	1	1893 —	205240	1902 —	385500
1885 —	19754	1894 —	224720	1903 —	402500
1886 —	40480	1895 —	246975	1904 —	420000
1887 —	64520	1896 —	268392	1905 —	447000
1888 —	90483	1897 —	291241	1906 —	471000
1889 —	116648	1898 —	311658	1907 —	494000
1890 —	141273	1899 —	331707	1908 —	519500
1891 —	163767	1900 —	351202	1909 —	550000
1892 —	185713	1901 —	368154		

Generally, "England" alone was used from 1870 to 1891. From that year on, stipulations of the McKinley Tariff Act required that goods imported into the United States from England bear the words, "Made in England." Articles so marked can usually be dated as originating from 1891, onward, but there are exceptions.

A big importer may order large quantities directly from England, and the individual pieces may not be marked.

Goods shipped today from England to Canada of modern bone china or semiporcelain will only say "England."

Goods not made for export, but bought by tourists in England, may not be marked.

Part of the fun in collecting is going to a big antique show and coming home with one good find. Such was the case of this set in typical shape of the early 1800s.

This early Staffordshire has the flanged top on the teapot and sugar and a broad lip on the creamer. The teapot and creamer handles curve up one-half inch higher than the top of the cover. The waste bowl is large in proportion to the set. Also included are two cups and saucers.

The design is of a white boy, with a hunter's bow, and a black boy standing side-by-side in the country.

Teapot height, 4 inches. Top of the handle, 4½ inches. Saucer diameter, 4½ inches. Blue decoration.

It is a difficult task trying to find true antique dishes (over 100 years old). This early English semiporcelain tea set with a flanged top on the teapot and sugar is decorated with a small floral sprig. The thickness of the semiporcelain is very finely executed and greatly resembles English Leeds ware.

The serving pieces were made in octagonal shapes circa 1830-1860. The waste bowl is extremely large compared to the rest of the set. The covers are over two inches tall.

This set includes a teapot and lid, covered sugar, creamer, waste bowl, serving plate, three cups, and four saucers.

Teapot height, 5½ inches. Plate diameter, 5 inches. Saucer diameter, 4½ inches.

On many unmarked sets, it sometimes is difficult to say tha this is from a certain country, dated a particular date, and mad of either earthenware or semiporcelain.

This is one of those sets. It is probably English circa 1840-1870. The set has some crazing and is decorated with a green, cable-stich-type design. The handles on the teapot and creamer are raised almost as high as the top of the flower finial The lip of the creamer spout is fairly wide. The saucers are deep dish style. The two handles on the sugar bowl are like small fans The set also includes two serving plates with small handles, four cups and saucers.

Teapot height, 4 ½ inches. Saucer diameter, 4 ½ inches. Serving pieces, including the handles, 6 inches.

Teapot height, 3 ¼ inches. Plate diameter, 4 ½ inches.

POMPADORE
H & K
(blue)

The "H & K" mark on this English set stands for Hackwood & Keeling, Market Street, Hanley.

This Staffordshire pottery made earthenwares in 1835-36. The name of the pattern is often included, and this set is called Pompadore, being an allover design of small blue flowers on a white background.

This tea set includes a bulbous teapot and cover, creamer, covered sugar, six plates, six cups, and six saucers.

IV—Earthenware
M—1859
R—August
2—Day 2
3—Parcel Number

Elsmore & Forster, Clayhills Pottery, Tunstall, England were the makers of this tea set. This Staffordshire pottery was in business from 1853 to 1871. In 1872 the name was changed to Elsmore (Thomas) & Son.

The impressed mark was registered August 2, 1859. Some o the features of this set that were typical of this date are its gray white color, its raised pattern, the crazing of the glaze, and the handleless cups.

This tea set is decorated with a raised wheat pattern and consists of a teapot and lid, covered sugar, creamer, six handleless cups, and six saucers.

Teapot height, 5 ½ inches. Saucer diameter, 4 ¼ inches.

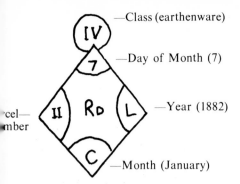

—Class (earthenware)

—Day of Month (7)

—Year (1882)

cel—
mber

—Month (January)

(black)

Teapot height, 3 ¼ inches.
Plate diameter, 4 ½ inches.

The transfer pattern of flowers, butterflies, and leaves was
ade by Ridgways, Bedford Works, Shelton, Hanley, England.
e archer's bow mark was registered in 1880. This pattern was
gistered in 1882.
Sepia (brown-toned) designs were a popular Victorian style.
onochromatic color schemes were commonly used on dishes
nineteenth century design.
This set includes a teapot and lid, creamer, open sugar bowl,
ur plates, four cups, and four saucers.

(blue)

Teapot height, 5 ½ inches. Plate diameter, 5 ½ inches.
Light blue decoration.

Brown, Westhead, Moore and Company succeeded the
dgways at Caldon Place, Shelton, England, in 1862 and
ntinued until 1920. They manufactured china of excellent
orkmanship and in the "contemporary" styles. The teapot,
eamer, and sugar have octagonal shapes. Some octagonal
apes go back to the 1840s.
This set includes a teapot and cover, creamer, covered sugar,
ste bowl, two plates, four cups, and four saucers. The pattern
me, Cord and Tassel, is printed on the mark. This mark was
ed circa 1862-1904.

(blue)

Rᵈ Nᵒ 25431
R.H.&S

R.H. & S. stands for the Staffordshire pottery owned by
lph Hammersley (& Son) Overhouse Pottery, Burslem,
gland.
The registration number 25431 would date this set 1885;
anley is the pattern name.
The most interesting features of this set are the footed teapot
d sugar bowl and the extremely large waste bowl. Footed
res were an early type design. The pieces are of white china
th a blue monochrome design of leaves, branches, flowers,
d birds.
Set consists of a teapot and lid, covered sugar, waste bowl, six
ps, five saucers, and six plates.

Teapot height, 4 ¼ inches. Plate diameter, 5 ¼ inches.

Teapot height, 5½ inches. Plate diameter, 5 inches.
(Courtesy of Dave and Jerry Krueger)

Two English companies (Old Hall Earthenware Co. Ltd., Old Hall Works; Hanley and Sampson Bridgwood & Son (LTD) Anchor Pottery, Longton) were known to make "opaque porcelain," which is a term for a special earthenware.

This particular impressed mark, with an E in the center for earthenware, does not indicate which manufacturer made this set circa 1885.

The orange design is of figures of portly little people in outdoor scenes. Pieces included are a teapot and lid, creamer, covered sugar, four plates, four cups, and four saucers.

Teapot height, 4½ inches. Plate diameter, 5 inches.

APPLE

(blue)

This Staffordshire pottery tea set was made by the British Anchor Pottery Co., Anchor Road, Longton, England.

This mark was used from 1884 to 1890. The pattern name is Apple, an allover apple design in blue. The set consists of a teapot and cover, sugar bowl with cover, waste bowl, six plates, six cups, and six saucers.

Re No 103739
(brown)

W & Co. were the initials for Whittaker and Co., Hallfield Pottery, Handley, England.

This Staffordshire pottery made earthenwares from 1886-1892. This nursery rhyme set was made in brown monochrome; the registry number (103739) dates this set 1888.

The teapot height is 4 inches and has "HEY DIDDLE DIDDLE THE CAT AND THE FIDDLE" as the subject of the design. The sugar bowl has "OLD MOTHER HUBBARD WENT TO THE CUPBOARD," and "THE FARMER'S WIFE JUMPED OUT OF BED" is on the creamer.

White tableware with blue trim was used from the beginning of china manufacturing in Europe. Blue was the most successful color to work with and was used in abundance on common ware items.

This English Mother Goose Nursery Rhymes set with a blue underglaze is almost like Flow Blue.

The only mark on this set is the English Garter mark on the face of the creamer; the mark is below and to the front of the spout. This should date the set between 1840 and 1870, or possibly to 1890.

The plates, saucers, and teapot have Mother Hubbard on them with dogs, rabbits, birds, and fish on the borders.

Old Mother Hubbard,
Went to the cupboard,
To get her poor dog a bone,
But when she got there,
The cupboard was bare,
And so her poor dog got none.

The cups and waste bowl have a dog, a bird, and a rabbit for decoration.

The covered sugar bowl has a boy fishing.

Little tommy Tittlemouse
Lived in a little house;
He caught fishes
In other men's ditches.

(blue)

The creamer has Mary and her lamb in school.

Mary had a little lamb
Its fleece was white as snow;
And everywhere that Mary went
The lamb was sure to go.

It followed her to school one day,
That was against the rule;
It made the children laugh and play
To see a lamb at school.

Gaudy Dutch was made as an English soft-paste with designs copied from Gaudy Oriental patterns. The name is from the Dutch Traders who first brought these wares to Europe from the Orient. These wares were produced in England circa 1800-1825 and didn't sell well so most of it was sent to the Pennsylvania Dutch communities.

The cobalt blue color is in the underglaze. The other colors were applied on top of the glaze, so they didn't wear well. No luster was applied.

Some of the better known patterns were Oyster, Tulip, Grape, Dahlia, Carnation, Double Rose, Single Rose, Urn, Butterfly, and War Bonnet.

Gaudy Welsh has similar patterns on semiporcelain, circa 1830-1850s, and used lusters, mostly in copper. It has more of a bluish purple coloring, contains a lot of cobalt color, and is more common than Gaudy Dutch.

Gaudy Ironstone was a heavier ware which contained limestone, circa 1855-1865. This ware has a blue underglaze with other colors applied on top and may or may not have had luster. Pieces are now scarce. Most of the Gaudy patterns didn't survive and are now rare and expensive.

Teapot height, 4 inches. Plate diameter, 5½ inches. Set of six with waste bowl. Blue decoration. (Also came in rose.)

Gaudy Welsh - Oyster pattern
Teapot height, 5¼ inches. Plate diameter, 5½ inches.

(Courtesy of Ruth Zalusky Thorstenson, Curator of the Hennepin County Historical Society Museum)

25

These four Staffordshire tea sets are believed to have bee[n] manufactured by Charles Allerton & Sons, Park Works, Longton, England. This factory began in 1831 and in 1912 became Allertons, Ltd. The sets pictured appear to have bee[n] made between 1887 and the early 1890s.

All four sets have similar characteristics. The figures are a[ll] amateurly drawn and look as if they could have been done by th[e] same person. The sets have a transfer picture in the center and [a] decorative border. The plates are all within 1/5th of an inch i[n] diameter of each other. Each plate is close to 5½ inches in diameter. The teapot and lid height of the first two sets is 5 ¼ inches and the height of the last two sets is 5 inches.

In finding these Staffordshire pieces in shops and antique shows, it appears that each of these sets was made originally in [a] choice of monochromatic designs and could be purchased in brown, blue, or rose.

(brown)

(brown)

(rose)

PUNCH
C. ALLERTON & SONS
ENGLAND
R° N°

(blue)

1. Design of a little girl with her arms around a big dog. Birds and flowers in the border. Set includes teapot, creamer, sugar, and four place settings.
2. A little girl sitting holding a cat with another cat drinking milk and a big dog sitting by her side. Birds and flowers in the background. This set consists of teapot, creamer, sugar, waste bowl, and six place settings.
3. A little girl standing with her apron full of flowers, flower m on the border. This set included a teapot, creamer, sugar, and four place settings.
4. Punch and Judy were either marionettes or puppets. Punch the nickname for the Italian, Punchinello. These were masked characters used in plays and entertainment at fairs. This set includes a teapot, creamer, sugar bowl, waste bowl, and four place settings. This is a Mother Goose nursery rhyme:

Punch and Judy
Fought for a pie;
Punch gave Judy
A knock in the eye.

Says Punch to Judy
Will you have any more?
Says Judy to Punch,
My eye is sore.

A tea leaf was considered good luck if you found it in your cup. Tea Leaf Luster was designed in the 1850s to dress up the plain white ironstone wares and was meant to give everybody good luck.

The tea leaf luster was usually applied in copper and, rarely, gold. The pattern on this set had a band of gold and a gold tea leaf in the center. The tea leaf was printed on the ironstone before it was glazed and fired, then the luster was hand-painted over the glaze.

Numerous Staffordshire potteries used this pattern with little variation and exported most of it to the United States. Because tea Leaf Luster was so popular, U.S. potteries also copied the design.

This tea set was made by Mellor, Taylor & Co., Burslem, England, with a printed mark dated from 1880 to 1904. The set includes a teapot and lid, covered sugar, and place settings for two.

(black)

RRANTED STONE CHINA
LLOR,TAYLOR & Cº
ENGLAND

Teapot height, 5½ inches. Plate diameter, 5 inches.

The Legend of the Plate

My willow-ware plate has a story,
  Pictorial, painted in blue,
From the land of the tea and tea plant,
  And the little brown man with the queue.
Whatever the Viands you're serving, Daughter
  Romance enters into the feast,
If you only pay heed to the legend,
  On the old china plate from the East.

Koong Shee was a mandarin's daughter
  And Chang was her lover, ah me
For surely her father's accountant
  Might never wed pretty Koong Shee.
So Chang was expelled from the compound,
  The lover's alliance to break,
And pretty Koong Shee was imprisoned
  In a little blue house by a lake.

The Doughty old mandarin reasoned
  It was time that his daughter should wed,
And the groom of his choosing should banish
  That silly romance from her head.
For years had great artists been stitching
  In symbols the dress she should wear,
Her head-band of scarlet lay waiting
  She should ride in a gold wedding chair.

He was busily plotting and planning
  When a message was brought him one day —
Young Chang had invaded the palace
  And taken his sweetheart away.
They were over the bridge when he saw them
  They were passing the big willow tree
And a boat at the edge of the water
  Stood waiting for Chang and Koong Shee.

The furious mandarin followed
  The groom with revenge in his eyes,
But the little boat danced on the water
  And traveled away with the prize.
When vengeance pursued to their shelter
  And burned the pagoda, they say,
From out of the flames rose the lovers —
  A pair of doves winging away.

And they flew toward the western heaven,
  The pretty Koong Shee and her Chang,
Or so says the famous old legend,
  From the land of the Yangtse Kiang;
I wouldn't be one to deny it,
  For the little blue dove and her mate
Forever are flying together,
  Across my old willow-ware plate.

—Author Unknown

(red)

The Willow pattern was designed by Thomas Minton in 17?
who adapted the pattern from Oriental export porcelain wa
that were blue and white Canton and Nanking wares brought
England from China. The Chinese called these pagoda scen
The Oriental Willows have a plain, simple design, while th
European and English Willows are much fussier and fanci
designs with complicated borders.

The Willow pattern was copied by numerous potters. Th
Staffordshire set was made by Edge Malkin & Co., Newp
and Middleport Potteries, Burslem (1870-1902).

This reddish, Willow pattern tea set with a teapot and l
creamer, sugar and lid, and waste bowl, has two cups, two
saucers, and two plates. This set has a matching soup tureer
inches high, that most likely came with a dinner service se

Teapot height, 4 inches. Plate diameter, 5 inches.

(green)

Teapot height, 5 ½ inches. Cup height, 2 ¼ inches.

This particular pattern is known as Blue Chelsea or Chelsea Sprig. It is a white china with blue decorations applied on the base and then glazed. This is a fine old pattern that goes back to George Washington's time.

Blue Chelsea has been made by many different manufacturers and also came in pinkish color.

This teapot and cup were made by Adderleys Ltd., Longton, England. This particular mark was used between 1912-1926. These are the only two pieces available to show. Sorry there isn't a full set.

Teapot height, 5 ¼ inches. Plate diameter, 4 ¾ inches.

If you are using a set of dishes for display in a small cupboard or as a setting with dolls, the design and scale will be more important than the mark. However, if you find a set of dishes, unmarked, and wish to identify them, you must consider texture and shape. This is a difficult area, and there is no one formula that can be followed.

This set, with many characteristics of English wares, including waste bowl, has quite a bit of crazing. It is believed to be from England, but it could have been made by a pottery company in the United States.

The serving pieces have unique shapes, more flat than round. The other pieces included, besides the waste bowl, are six plates, six cups, and six saucers.

Williamsburg

(purple luster)

Williamsburg sets were made in England and sold there or in Canada in the 1920s and 1930s. These sets resemble English Sprig wares that were pink and purple luster with sprig-and-floral-type designs.

One coat of copper luster solution painted on creamy white miniporcelain comes out pink; a second coat will make it come out purple.

This set includes a teapot and lid, open sugar, creamer, six cups, and six saucers.

Teapot height, 5 inches. Saucer diameter, 4 ¼ inches.

This Royal Doulton, Lambeth, England, tea service was made by Doulton with impressed marks.

Lambeth Doulton preceded all the other Doultons. These pieces have been put together as a set, but the marks are different and may have been made at different times. These pieces are not necessarily children's pieces, they may have been individual serving pieces.

The small open dish has the circular impressed mark without the crown or lion. The creamer and sugar have the impressed mark with the crown and lion that originated in 1902. The small teapot has impressed mark "Doulton, Lambeth, England," which was used from 1891 to 1956.

The set is a finely made, salt-glazed stoneware. The coloring is dark brown on the top half and light brown on the bottom half. Raised designs of English flavor such as the horse and hounds and Englishman sitting with a pipe, an Englishman sitting with a tankard of ale, trees, and a windmill appear on the bottom half of the pieces. The height of the teapot is 4¼ inches.

French hard porcelain has a fine glaze, is nonporous and has a white, opaque body. The kaolin (white clay ingredient) is molded and fired at a high temperature. Then the glaze is applied and fired at a still higher temperature. This fuses the glaze onto the body to give a very delicate looking, translucent porcelain. The spoilage in this method is three or four times higher than that of the English method, thus making it more expensive.

The Limoges District, France, is noted for having this pure kaolin, and has produced quality porcelain similar to that originally produced in China.

It is difficult finding these French tea sets. This set is a pure white with heavy gold trim and a fancy, swirl-type finial (the decorative top on the covers). Included in this set is a teapot and cover, creamer, covered sugar, two cups, and two saucers.

The French tea sets have been especially difficult for me to find until recently. Ironically, two sets have appeared in different parts of the country. Both were in the original box with similar lithographed covers. The style of dress on these boxes would date them about 1880 or 1890.

After carefully checking the boxes, it appears that both sets sold for $1, each. Probably some French sets seen today are misattributed to other countries because they were made as inexpensive playthings, thus accounting for the poorer quality. These French sets are a very white porcelain with uneven shapes. The decoration is hand-painted flowers and gold trim. Each set contains a teapot and sugar, both with fancy covers, creamer, six plates, six cups, and six saucers.

Teapot height, 4 inches. Saucer diameter, 3 ¼ inches. Circa 1870.

Smaller sets, teapot height, 3 ½ inches. Plate diameter, 2 ½ inches.

Larger sets, teapot height, 4 inches. Plate diameter, 3 ½ inches.

33

Many German play dishes, prior to 1900, were not marked at all, or just marked "Germany" for the country origin.

Some of the favorite topics for decorating play dishes are scenes of children at play, faces of children, scenes from nursery rhymes, and pictures of various animals.

German dishes also used luster in their trim. Pink was the most used color. Lusters in blue to blue-gray to gray-green were also used, as were yellow and mother-of-pearl.

The makers of these toy dishes intended them to be played with and would have been surprised to know that they have survived for nearly a century.

Several manufacturers produced undecorated white china that was either sold for use as whiteware or sold to other companies to be decorated. Consequently, the collector, today, may find a confusing mixture; that is, the same decals may appear on differing china shapes. Some pieces in a set may not be marked and there is a wide range of quality, from very fine with perfectly placed decals to rather poor with flaws and bumps, crooked decals, and uneven shapes. This casual inconsistency was acceptable because the dishes were intended solely as playthings.

Germany must have exported tons of children's play dishes in varying styles and shapes. The servers could be used for either tea or coffee, although coffee would usually have been served in Germany. The United States would serve either tea or coffee.

Children's play dishes don't always hold true to shapes, so try to accept sets being called tea sets when the pot may be shaped more like a coffee server.

When little girls had a party it would usually be referred to as a tea party regardless of what beverage was served.

Villeroy & Boch (V & B) was founded in 1836 when Eugene Francis Boch in Mettlach and Nicholas Villeroy in Wallerfangen, Germany, became partners. Since that time and until 1926 they added factories at nine other locations in Germany. The V & B mark is used for this chain of factories. V & B is the maker of the famous Mettlach steins.

This is a nicely made tea set that consists of a teapot and cover, creamer, covered sugar, six plates, six cups, and six saucers.

(blue)

Pattern, Paula. Teapot height, 5¾ inches. Plate diameter, 5 inches. Decorated in blue.

This German porcelain tea set is decorated with children, a favorite topic in play dishes. The children are dressed in styles of early 1900. The little girls' dresses are knee-length and the hair is cut shorter. They were still wearing puffy hats.

There are five scenes on this set of dishes. They are: two girls holding up a doll; a boy and girl in party clothes; the boy helping the girl with her cape; a boy and girl in the same party clothes with their coats off, kissing; a boy pulling a girl in a homemade wooden wagon; and a boy and girl sliding on a sled past a snowman.

This set consists of a teapot and cover, creamer, covered sugar, six plates, six cups and saucers.

BAVARIA

(gold)

Teapot height, 5 inches. Plate diameter, 4¾ inches.

Bavaria is in southern Germany bordered by Austria on the south and Czechoslovakia on the east. Sets of dishes marked "Bavaria" are believed to have come from the area around Nurnberg. Kaolin or clay is found around the town of Amberg (less than fifty miles west of Nurnberg) and near the town of Bayreuth (less than fifty miles north of Nurnberg).

This set has various scenes of a boy and girl picking flowers. The boy is dressed in pantaloons and a large puffy hat. The girl has a plain dress with the skirt length below the knees, puffed sleeves, and a hat. These styles were worn by children in the 1890s.

Set includes a teapot and cover, creamer, covered sugar, six cups, and six saucers.

Teapot height, 5¼ inches. Saucer diameter, 4¼ inches.

Teapot height, 5 ¼ inches. Saucer diameter, 4 ¼ inches.

A German porcelain tea set, circa 1900, was designed from the Mother Goose nursery rhyme, "This Is the House That Jack Built."

The set consists of a teapot and cover, creamer, covered sugar, six cups, and six saucers. Here is the last verse of that rhyme.

> *This is the horse and the hound and the horn,*
> *That belonged to the farmer sowing his corn,*
> *That kept the cook that crowed in the morn,*
> *That waked the priest all shaven and shorn,*
> *That married the man all tattered and torn,*
> *That kissed the maiden all forlorn,*
> *That milked the cow with the crumpled horn,*
> *That tossed the dog,*
> *That worried the cat,*
> *That killed the rat,*
> *That ate the malt*
> *That lay in the house that Jack built.*

Teapot height, 5 inches. Plate diameter, 6 inches.

Quaint German tea set, circa 1900, has four different rhymes. A complete rhyme is on each plate. The first half of the same rhyme is on the matching cup with the second half on the saucer. The first half of "Jack and Jill" is on the creamer, the second half of the rhyme is on the large open sugar. "Hey Diddle Diddle" is on the back of the teapot.

This tea set is exceptionally large. Little children could eat from the plates. The mugs are as large as child-sized. Here are the rhymes on the set.

> *Jack and Jill went up the hill*
> *To fetch a pail of water,*
> *Jack fell down and broke his crown*
> *And Jill came tumbling after.*
>
> *HEY, diddle diddle! the cat and the fiddle,*
> *The cow jumped over the moon,*
> *The little dog laughed to see such sport,*
> *And the dish ran away with the spoon.*
>
> *Little Miss Muffet sat on a tuffet*
> *Eating of curds and whey,*
> *There came a great spider and sat down beside her*
> *And frightened Miss Muffet away.*
>
> *Humpty Dumpty sat on a wall*
> *Humpty Dumpty had a great fall,*
> *And all the king's horses and all the king's men*
> *Couldn't put Humpty Dumpty together again.*

Some children's dishes were designed in the shapes of birds or animals for novelty-type wares.

Teapots and cream pitchers have been molded as a whole animal with the spout being the mouth of the figure.

Bird heads with the beaks pointing up are the finial designs on the covers of this white German porcelain set. The only other trims are gold bands and gold beaks. The sugar bowl handles are in the shape of bird heads. The set includes a teapot and cover, creamer, covered sugar, four plates, four cups, and four saucers.

Teapot height, 5½ inches.
Plate diameter, 4¾ inches.
(Courtesy of Dave and Jerry Krueger)

Notice the delicate designs of the serving pieces. This is a finely made china set with pink bands. Includes four plates, four cups and four saucers.

German circa 1870. Teapot height, 4½ inches. Plate diameter, 4¾ inches.

This German tea set has extremely large plates, cups, and saucers in relation to the sizes of the teapot, creamer, and sugar. This is a mediocre-quality set that was intended for little girls to use.

German circa 1890. Teapot height, 5½ inches. Plate diameter, 6¼ inches. Set of six place settings.

German circa 1890. Teapot height, 6 inches. Plate diameter, 5 inches. Set of four place settings.

This would be considered either a tea or coffee set. The handles are very decorative and the plates are child's play-size.

(black)

German circa 1890. Teapot height, 5¼ inches. Plate diameter, 5¼ inches. Set of six place settings.

Chicken decals and bluish-gray luster edges were both popular features in German dishes.

GERMANY
279

(red)

German circa 1890. Teapot height, 4½ inches. Saucer diameter, 4½ inches. Set of two — no plates.

German porcelain tea set in pink luster has an unusual sugar bowl with a fluted top. Pieces are decorated with a flower design.

German circa 1890. Teapot height, 5 inches. Saucer diameter, 4½ inches. Set of two — no plates. Creamy color.

An example of German porcelain made more in the French style. The scenes are of a Victorian man and woman. The cups and serving pieces are all footed.

Pictured is a particularly unique grouping, because it is made of actually a coffee set and a tea set in the same pattern. It is marked "Germany" in red letters and it would appear to date ca 1880s.

The pieces are all white and decorated with small flowers. All have a blue ring around the edge. Both sets have four place settings.

Coffee pot height, 4 inches. Teapot height, 2¾ inches. Both creamers, 3 inches. Both sugars, 2¾ inches. Coffee plate diameter, 4¾ inches. Tea plate diameter, 4½ inches. Coffee saucer diameter, 3¾ inches. Tea saucer diameter, 3½ inches.

This German porcelain tea set with decals of big, red roses is a revival of Victorian rococo shapes and was probably done in the early 1900s.

The cups are fascinating because they are shaped more like cocoa cups than teacups. The set includes a teapot and cover, creamer, covered sugar, six plates, and six cups and saucers.

Teapot height, 4 inches. Plate diameter, 5¼ inches.

Pattern name, Maria. Teapot height, 6 inches. Saucer
diameter, 4 inches.

(green)

Philip Rosenthal of Selb, Germany, established a porcelain
factory in 1879. Coffee and tea sets were produced on a large
scale since 1891. Rosenthal porcelain is carefully modeled and
decorated and would be compared with the best manufactured
in Germany.

This Rosenthal set is twentieth century of an extremely fine
quality and is decorated with petite flowers. The cups are footed
and have graceful designs of flowers on both the outside and
inside of the cups. Set includes a teapot, six cups and saucers.

Teapot height, 2¾ inches. Plate diameter, 3 inches.

The most interesting thing about the "Miss Muffet Tea Set"
is the box. The picture on the box is marked "Germany" and the
style of the little girls' dresses and hair would date it as about
1920-30s.

The dishes are a porcelain with gold-painted bands and five
red dots in a half-circle for decoration. The set includes a teapot
and cover, creamer, covered sugar, four plates, four cups, and
four saucers.

A cabaret set is a tea set which has a matching tray to serve [tea].

The German luster tea set has a uniform tray that measures [?]⁄2 by 6 ½ inches. The teapot height is 3 ½ inches.

The blue-to-shaded-yellow porcelain set has a tray, 9 ¼ by 8 ¼ [in]ches, that was handmade in freeform. The teapot has a [fo]rmed handle across the top. The teapot height is 4 ½ inches [in]cluding the handle.

Shell and coral is the pattern on this fine porcelain set. The [se]t is pink on the bottom and gradually shades to white at the [to]p. The centers of the covers are also pink. The decorations also [in]clude a gold band on the covers, gold spatter on the handles, [sp]out, and on the shell finials. The teapot height is 4 ¼ inches.

Dishes marked Nippon were produced for export only fro
approximately 1890 to 1915. Noritake china is produced by th
Nihon (Japan) Toki (Chinawear) Kaisna (Company) factory
Nagoya, Japan. This factory was established in 1904 for th
purpose of exporting. Many items are hand painted and mark
accordingly. Large quantities of Japanese play dishes were
imported between 1918 and 1941 and, again, after the end
World War II in 1945. Japan continues to make china tea se
usually marked "Made in Japan," and exports them to the
United States in quantity.

The Blue Willow pattern is one of the best-known Japane
patterns found in children's play dishes. They have been made
a variety of sizes. This pattern basically is the mandarin's
pagoda, the willow tree, the bridge, the runaway lovers, the bo
that took them to their island, and the doves they turned int

The factories that made tea sets for export quite often ma
dinner serving pieces to match. Some pieces included are sou
tureen, platter, covered vegetable dish, gravy boat, and cak
plate.

Japanese sets varied from fair to fine, but generally were
mediocre quality. Remember, these sets were made as toys a
priced accordingly. They were intended to be played with an
therefore, are easily distinguished from other fine children's se

At a glance this tea set would give the impression that it is [Ge]rman, both in design and texture, but the bottom is flat and [po]rous, a definite look of Japanese. This set appears to have [be]en made in the late 1800s.

Teapot height, 4 ½ inches. Saucer diameter, 3 ½ inches. Set of six — no plates.

Teapot height, 3 ½ inches. Saucer diameter, 4 inches. Set of two.

[T]his set is marked "JAPAN" in black letters. Note the large [siz]e of the cups in relation to the rest of the set. The bottom of [the] teapot is not glazed.

Nippon rising sun mark. Teapot height, 3½ inches. Plate diameter, 4¼ inches. Set of six — hand-painted scenes of children.

This tea set seems to be from the same mold as the set above, but has the Noritake mark. Set of four, covered dish, and platter.

This tea set has the same Noritake mark as the above set but is a finer quality. Teapot height, 3¼ inches. Plate diameter, 3½ inches. Set of six. Pink with black trim.

Noritake made numerous sets of children's dishes of exceptionally fine quality. The mark on this set is the same as the two preceding sets.

This tea set is a cream color with light blue, lace-type trim and blue bands. The flowers are soft but colorful. Included with the pot, creamer, and sugar are six place settings.

Teapot height, 4 inches.
Plate diameter, 4¾ inches.
(Courtesy of Dave and Jerry Krueger)

The Blue Willow pattern was made in many sizes. Some of the extra pieces include platter, covered vegetable, and gravy boat, besides the regular tea service of six place settings.

Blue Willow pattern, "Made in Japan." Teapot height, 4 inches. Plate diameter, 4¼ inches.

This porcelain, toy tea set called "Classic Blue Bird Design" was made by Yamada Toshio, Shoten, Japan, and was sold by Sears Roebuck & Co. circa 1940.

Teapot height, 4 inches. Plate diameter, 4 inches. Set of six place settings.

Teapot height, 4¼ inches. Saucer diameter, 3½ inches. Set of two — no plates.

A silhouette is usually a profile portrait made on the outline of a person's shadow. These silhouette images against a light background show children playing with Japanese lanterns. The handle on the teapot gives the effect of bamboo. These designs are now considered Art Deco and are very popular.

Teapot height, 4½ inches. Plate diameter, 5 inches. "Made in Japan."

This tea set of six place settings also includes a cake plate, covered vegetable dish, platter, and gravy boat.

"Made in Japan." Teapot height, 4¼ inches. Plate diameter, 4½ inches.

Pictured is a tea set with four place settings that is typically Japanese in both shape and pattern.

The Moss Rose pattern creates an interesting set because of e extra serving pieces. This set includes a teapot, creamer, gar bowl, six plates, six cups and saucers, a cake plate, platter, vered serving dish, and salt and pepper shakers.

JAPAN

(blue) or (red)

Plate diameter, 4½ inches. Cake plate diameter, 6¼ inches.

This rose pattern is not as fancy as the Moss Rose. The tea set nsists of six place settings.

This set and the preceding three sets are typical of the types of shes made in the 1940s.

Same mark as above in black. Teapot height, 3½ inches. Plate diameter, 4 inches.

Lusters or iridescent glazes were quite popular in the 1930s. The blossom set is a green-gray luster, and the three-place-setting doll dish set is a caramel to green luster.

(red)

Left: teapot height, 3½ inches. Saucer diameter, 3¾ inches. Set of four — no plates. Right: teapot height, 3 inches. Saucer diameter, 3¼ inches. Set of three — no plates.

Teapot height, 3½ inches. Plate diameter, 3¾ inches.

This little Japanese china set is decorated with scenes picturing a little girl riding her rooster-pulled chariot or holding a fishing pole and a fish. This type of work was done in the 1940s. The later Japanese transfer patterns have a thicker, heavier paint.

This is a dinner set with extra serving pieces including a covered bowl, platter, gravy pitcher, small open bowl, and a salt dish, plus the usual pieces of a teapot, four plates, four cups and saucers.

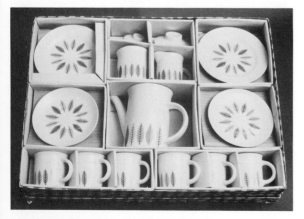

Teapot height, 4¾ inches. Plate diameter, 4½ inches.

A contemporary style marked "Made in Japan" was produced circa 1950. This is a tea service with six place settings.

The pattern of Thousand Faces china has concentric rows of ttle faces which represent Buddhist saints preparing to become ɹddhas. They form part of the border design.

The colorful center represents the bright Buddhist robes, lack, blue, orange, green, yellow). Orange is the edominating color. It is on the border, the concentric rings tween the rows of faces, six times in the robe, and in the nter.

The piece pictured is twentieth century. Older pieces have a ore intricate design. This type has been seen in demitasse sets, t it is questionable if it was used for play dishes. The saucer own is 4½ inches in diameter.

(red)

Japanese doll dishes often came boxed in a set of three place tings.

This little poem is on the box of the doll face set.

DOLLY TEA SET
Here's a tea set for your
dolly and for you
And greetings for you both
go with it, too.

Teapot height, 2¾ inches. Saucer diameter, 2 inches. Set of three, Doll Face patterns.

Teapot height, 2¼ inches. Saucer diameter, 2¼ inches. Set of three in Dragon decor. Circa 1950.

Sears, Roebuck & Co., Chicago

Fall and Winter, 1927-1928

From the description of luster and style of shapes, these set: could all have been made in Japan.

Everything for Tea

Beautiful 21-Piece Luster Edge China Tea Set, $2.98

Our Finest Quality Set. Almost like mother's in size and quality. A large purchase and the elimination of an expensive display box make this value possible. Latest style creamer and sugar. Pink rose and pale blue luster decorations. Handles on all pieces, and spout of teapot luster finish. Six 5-inch plates, six 4⅛-inch saucers, six 2⅞-inch cups, 5¾x4-inch teapot, 4⅛x2¾-inch sugar and 3⅛x2-inch creamer. Shipping weight, 5 pounds.
49K1620..................................$2.98

9-Piece Set for 49c

Not the awkward looking pieces usually offered at this price but pieces like sister's, well shaped and finished in high glaze finish. Has latest pretty flower decorations of black leaves and stripes and light yellow border on all pieces; saucers striped in black and yellow. Has three 3¼-inch saucers, three 2¼-inch cups, 4¼x3⅝-inch teapot, 2¾x2⅝-inch sugar, 2 9/16x1⅞-inch creamer. Shipping weight, 1¾ lbs.
49K1624.......................49c

This Beautiful Set for Only $1.98
21 Pieces Fine Quality China

This set would delight any little girl with its beautiful ros design and trimmed edge tan luster finish. All handles luster fin ished as is the spout on teapot and all the covers with set. A beautiful as some of the big sets offered. Six 4¼-inch plates; si 3 11/16-inch saucers; six 2½-inch cups; 5¼x4 5/16-inch teapot; 3¼x3 inch sugar and 2⅝x2⅛-inch creamer. Shpg. wt., 4 lbs.
49K1636....................................$1.98

11-Piece Set for 79c

All parts glazed which insures smooth finish; child cannot cut self as on cheaper quality sets on market. This pretty set has design surrounded with gilt lattice design; all edges have tan luster border set off with gold stripe. Four 2¼-inch cups; four 3⅛-inch saucers; 4½x3¾-inch teapot; 3x9/16-inch sugar and 2⅛x1⅞-inch creamer. Shipping weight, 1¾ pounds.
49K1623....................... 79c

Our Leader Value! 21 Pieces $1.59

Girls! Imagine this pretty little set of good grade glazed china on your table all ready for dolly's party. Has the popular broad bottom teapot, sugar bowl and creamer. Each piece is trimmed with pale blue band and decorated with pink roses encircled with fancy brown design. Very attractive set. Six 4⅛-inch plates; six 3-inch saucers; six 2¼-inch cups; teapot, 4⅞ inches wide by 3 inches high over all. Sugar and creamer in proportion. Shipping weight, 3¾ pounds.
49K1631..$1.59

15-Piece Set for 98c

Good grade glazed china set with we shaped pieces. Has pink rose and gilt tri design; blue and gilt stripes set off the pa green body color. Six 2¼-inch cups; si 3⅛-inch saucers; 4⅝x3¾-inch teapot; 2¾ 2⅝-inch sugar and 2x1⅞-inch creamer. A pieces have full green border. Shipping wt 2¾ pounds.
49K1622......................... 98c

It is not known if Mexican tea sets have been made in children's playtime dishes, however, tiny miniature sizes are available.

This demitasse-sized cup and saucer is a good grade of Mexican pottery with a fine glaze. "Mexico" is written on the bottom, under the glaze. Saucer diameter is 4¼ inches.

The two small dishes are not well cured and are very brittle. These two pieces probably have a lead glaze and are not safe for food. These pieces have an impressed mark "Made in Mexico." The small bowl's diameter is 2¼ inches, the larger bowl's diameter is 2¾ inches.

MEXICO

N⁰ 6.

(red)

Teapot height, 3½ inches. Saucer diameter, 4¼ inches.

The Gardner porcelain factory was established in 1754 by an Englishman, Frances Gardner, who had come to Moscow, Russia, eight years earlier.

The factory produced tea and coffee sets and remained in the family until 1891 when it was sold to M. S. Kuznetsov.

Russian porcelain is usually a heavy porcelain with bright colors and gaudy patterns; however, this set has a look of being cosmopolitan rather than Russian.

This set is a delicate pastel blue with petite, hand-painted flowers and porcelain bows at the top of the handles. The quality is such that it could have belonged to an aristocratic family. It was made by the Gardner Factory during the rein of Alexander the III dating from 1881 to 1894. The pieces included are a teapot and cover, creamer, sugar bowl, four cups and four saucers.

The Langenthal porcelain factory in Berne, Switzerland, began production in 1906. They produced this finely made porcelain set decorated with petite red roses, green leaves, and gold band trim.

The creamer is almost as large as the tea- or coffeepot, or this might have been made as a cocoa pot. Strong coffee may be diluted with an equal quantity of hot milk to produce "café au lait." The sugar bowl is handleless, as are the six cups. Also included are six saucers. Handleless cups were in vogue around 1800 in Europe. It is surprising to find cups made this way after 1900.

Teapot height, 4 inches. Creamer height, 3 inches. Saucer diameter, 3½ inches.

(black)

American Depression glass was produced as an inexpensiv[e] glassware for everyday use and was mainly made in the 1930s. [A] small amount appeared in the late 1920s and some companie[s] continued making it into the 1940s.

This glass was made in pink, green, blue, amber, and crysta[l.] In some cases glassware of this period was also produced in dar[k] colors.

Children's Depression glass sets are hard to find. To my knowledge there were only five glass companies that made children's Depression glass sets. American companies did produce children's china sets, but these are also hard to find[.]

Sears Roebuck & Co. Catalog

(1902 Edition)

Toy China Tea Sets.

No. 29R377 Toy China Tea Set, consists of cups, saucers, teapot, sugar bowl and creamer, about 16 pieces, small 25-cent value packed in paper box. Per set 15c

Shipping weight, 10 ounces.

No. 29R379 Toy China Tea Set, consisting of decorated plates, cups, saucers, tea pot, creamer, sugar bowl, about 23 pieces. Price, per set.............25c

Shipping weight, 20 ounces.

No. 29R381 Toy China Tea Set, consisting of about 17 pieces, decorated plates, cups, saucers, tea pot, creamer and sugar bowl. Larger size, and very interesting for a child. Splendid 75-cent value.
Price, per set....... ....50c

Shipping weight, 48 ounces.

No. 29R383 Toy China Tea Set, consisting of about 25 pieces, finely decorated plates, cups, saucers, tea pot, creamer and sugar bowl. Large size and extra value. Price, per set................ ....75c

Shipping weight, 56 ounces.

No. 29R385 Toy China Tea Set, consisting of about 25 pieces, decorated cups, saucers, plates, tea pot, creamer and sugar bowl. Our larger size set, and suitable for misses up to 14 or 15 years of age. **Unmailable on account of weight.**
Price, per set......................................$1.00

Shipping weight, 7 pounds.

No. 29R387 Toy China Tea Set. This, our finest set, consists of 23 pieces finely decorated cups, saucers, plates, teapot, creamer, sugar bowl, etc., larger cups and saucers, and suitable for young misses for an afternoon tea. Equal to any $2.00 value.
Price, per set....................................$1.40

Shipping weight, 9 pounds.

K.T.&K. are the initials for Knowles, Taylor and Knowles
o., East Liverpool, Ohio.
The pottery plant was begun in 1854 by Issac W. Knowles and
sac A. Harvey. Issac W. Knowles became sole proprietor and,
1870, formed a partnership with John N. Taylor and Homer
Knowles. Knowles, Taylor, & Knowles Co. was incorporated
der this name in 1891.
This set is a plain white ironstone china with the only
corations being a gold band. The set consists of a teapot and
d, creamer, covered sugar, four plates, four cups, and four
ucers.

Teapot height, 5½ inches.
Plate diameter, 4¾ inches.
(Courtesy of Dave and Jerry Krueger)

(black)

Pictured is an ironstone china tea set made by the Wheeling
ttery Co., Wheeling, West Virginia. The set has two marks.
e first mark was used from 1880 to 1886 and the second mark
s used from 1886 to 1896. It seems reasonable to assume that
s set was made in 1886 when the company was in the process
changing the mark.
All the decorating of the old Moss Rose pattern were hand-
inted. It is quite unusual to find an American set with a waste
wl. This usually makes me think it could be English or that
e factory was run by an Englishman.
The ironstone tea set includes a teapot and cover, creamer,
vered sugar, waste bowl, and place settings for four; plates,
ps, and saucers.

(black)

(black)

Teapot height, 5¾ inches. Plate diameter, 5 inches.

Teapot height, 3¾ inches. Plate diameter, 5½ inches.
Saucer diameter, 4¾ inches.

The United States Pottery Co. began in 1899, in Wellsville, Ohio, and was the maker of this semiporcelain tea set. This style dates in the early 1900s. There is quite a bit of crazing and some of the decals show wear on this sample.

The characters represented on these dishes are very similar to the children on a German set in the coffee section. The children's activities represent football, baseball, roller skating, leapfrog and dice rolling.

The shapes were a unique design. The teapot height with cover is 3¾ inches and is as big around as a saucer in this set. Other pieces are a creamer, covered sugar, four plates, four cups, and four saucers.

(black)

FLORENCE
COOK POTTERY CO.

FLORENCE

Teapot height, 3¾ inches. Plate diameter, 6 inches.
Platter size, 6¾ by 8½ inches.

Another difficult area in the search for children's play dishes is in American pottery or semiporcelain sets.

It was fun finding this typically American set, circa 1900, made by the Cook Pottery Company, Trenton, New Jersey. The dealer who had this set assured me it was bought at a department store in St. Paul, Minnesota, in 1905.

Americans are noted for serving tea or coffee with their meal, thus the reason for for cups and saucers plus dinner serving pieces in the same set. This set is large, and little girls would have been able to eat a meal at their own table.

The set includes thirty-four pieces. They are: a teapot and cover, creamer, covered sugar, six plates, six cups and saucers, six individual bowls, one platter, one covered dish, and two open serving dishes.

The pattern is called "Florence" and is a design of two little girls in three separate poses.

ro Agate
arksburg, West Virginia

The trademark stands for "As A Kro Flies," a crow flying
ough the letter A. The crow is carrying an agate in its beak
d one in each claw.

Most Akro Agate pieces will bear the trademark. The
hiquita" pattern may be marked "J.P." These sets were
oduced for the J. Pressman Co. of New York.

The children's dishes were manufactured mainly between
40 and 1948. The Akro Agate sets have four different kinds of
ss using all the colors of the rainbow:

Transparents or clear
Enamel baked on glass
Opaque solid colors
Opaque, two-color, marbleized

The tea sets were boxed in all one color or mixed colors. These
s range from six pieces to twenty-eight pieces. The water sets
re usually boxed with four or six glasses and a water pitcher.
e water pitcher has straight sides, whereas the teapot curves in
he base. The cup handles were usually wing-shaped in design.
e individual patterns of the tea sets are described in the
lowing pages.

iquita — solid opaques, transparent glass, baked on enamel.
ne-shaped, four circular rings border cup and plates; five or
rings on the teapot; wing-tip handles.

ncentric Rib — solid opaques. Six close ribs on plate, saucer,
d cup. No bands on the handles. Horizontal discs with five
tical, grated ribbons on the serving pieces.

ncentric Ring — solid opaques, transparent glass. Six rings,
e concentric rib except the band is wider. Horizontal discs go
und the handles; five vertical ribbons, eighteen vertical panels
the inside; wing-tip handles.

cal — solid opaques. Footed teapot, creamer, sugar, and
s. The decal is a row of five pink flowers with green leaves
und the flowers. Handles are open.

erior Panel — opaques solid and marbleized, transparent
ss. Outside plain; serving pieces with or without ribbons.
ide small size, eighteen panels — five ribbons. Inside larger
e, sixteen panels — seven ribbons. Plate exterior has vertical
nels of sixteen or eighteen; underside is plain.

tagonal — opaques solid and marbleized. Eight-sided, small
d large sizes. Large saucer is the same as the small plate.
ng-tip handles.

tagonal O — Same as pattern above except the handles are
en.

ised Daisy — solid opaques. Small size. Raised daisies
und band of the plates and on the teapot. Wing-tip handles.

cked Disc — solid opaques. Serving pieces have horizontal
cs and five ribbons. Cup has horizontal discs. Plate and
cer have six concentric ribs; wing-tip handles.

Stacked Disc and Panel — solid opaques, transparent glass Serving pieces close to stacked disc with rings around wing-handles and interior paneled. Plate and saucer exterior hav vertical bands; base has three rings.

Stippled Band — transparent glass. All pieces plain except small band of stippling.

Stippled Interior Panel — transparent glass. Exterior pieces li stippled band. Interior pieces like interior panel.

Water sets consisting of pitcher and tumblers were made match some of the patterns. They are: Interior Panel (large si Octagonal and Octagonal-O (large size); Stacked Disc (sma size); Stacked Disc and Panel (large size); Stippled Band (la size); Stippled Interior Panel (small size).

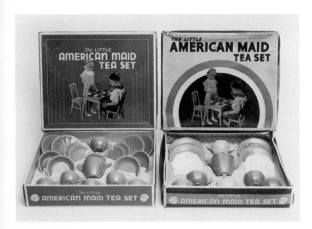

Left: green Interior Panel — large size. Right: blue, white, yellow — Octagonal.

Row 1   Blue Stacked Disc and Panel.

Row 2   Green Interior Panel — small size.

Row 3   Marbleized Agate — lemonade and oxblood Octagonal.

Row 4   Water glasses and pitchers.

eral Glass Co.
umbus, Ohio...

Diana pattern was produced in crystal or pink in the years
7-1941.

he junior set includes six plates, and six cups and saucers
cer 4 ½ inches in diameter). This set came with a stand that
l the plates and saucers and had hooks for the cups.
here is some question if this set was produced as a child's set
if it was intended to be a demitasse set.
he toy mugs are one-ounce size and came in crystal, pink,
en, and amber. They were produced in the late 1930s and
e the trademark stamped on the bottom.

zel Atlass Glass Co.
eeling, West Virginia...

Vedding Band pattern was produced in the 1940s. The sets of
y dishes were a white opaque glass with fired-on colors. There
e pastel shades in pink, blue, green, and yellow.
his set included fourteen pieces; four plates (5 ¼ inches in
meter), four cups, four saucers, one creamer, and one sugar.
box was marked "Little Hostess Party Set."

wentieth Century pattern was either white opaque glass or
te opaque glass with fired-on colors. The colors were pastel
the Wedding Band pattern, but the size was a little larger, a
te being six inches in diameter. This fourteen-piece set was
led "Party Set."
3oth of these sets also came in dark colors (black, maroon,
y, and shades of yellow, green and blue) with a teapot and
er.

Cherry Blossom — pink

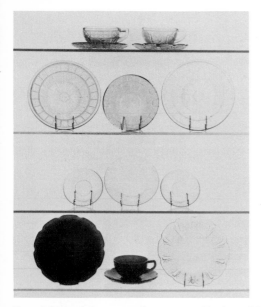

Row 1 Two pink cups and saucers — Doric and Pansy, Cherry Blossom. Row 2 Doric and Pansy — teal plate and saucer; pink plate. Row 3 Homespun — pink saucer and plate; clear saucer. Row 4 Cherry Blossom — delfite plate, cup, and saucer; pink plate.

Jeannette Glass Co.
Jeannette, Pennsylvania..

Cherry Blossom pattern was produced in pink and delfite, the years 1930-1939. (Delfite is a soft, opaque blue color.) Th box was marked "Jeannette Junior Dinner Set."

The set has four plates (six inches in diameter), four cups, fo saucers (4 ½ inches in diameter), one creamer, and one suga The complete set has fourteen pieces.

These pieces are being reproduced, so be careful when buying To identify an old piece, hold a cup in your right hand by t handle and make sure the cherries hang from the stem.

Doric and Pansy pattern is found in pink and teal (ultramarine) in the years 1937-1938. They were boxed as "Pretty Polly Party Dishes." The sizes are the same as Cher Blossom and they also came as a fourteen-piece set.

Homespun pattern appears in pink and crystal in the year 1938-1940.

This set also had fourteen pieces, but a different combinatio The set had four plates (4 ½ inches in diameter), four cups, fo saucers (3 ¼ inches in diameter), one teapot and cover.

McKee Glass Co.
Jeanette, Pennsylvania

Laurel pattern tea sets were produced in the 1935-1940 era The sets were made in white opal, French ivory, or jade gree There were also two styles of edges, either smooth or scallope and may or may not have a fired-on, colored band in red, orange, green, or black.

The sets were called "Hostess Tea Set" and the best know design in this pattern is the Scottie Dog which was applied by stamping process.

These sets consisted of fourteen pieces; four plates (six inch in diameter), four cups, four saucers (4 ½ inches in diameter one creamer, and one sugar.

At this point it should be helpful to know the types of
children's play dishes that are being manufactured by American
companies today.

1976-Chilton Toys,
Aluminum Specialty Co.
Manitowoc, Wisconsin 54220

In 1923 Chilton introduced aluminum toy sets with names c
Wonderland, Kiddyland, and Kiddykook. A new line of plasti
was added in 1958.

Here are a few of the sets being manufactured by this
company.

"Revere" Ware — made to match the real and well-known
copper bottomed cookware.

"Corning" Ware — the same shapes and styling as mother's

Plastic Tea Sets — this includes many shapes, sizes, and desigr
from two to six place settings. Some of the pattern names a
Bicentennial, Bluebird, First Love, Fire Flower, Formal, Tuli
and Daisy.

Aluminum Sets — pots and pans; cookware and bakeware.

"Teflon" — cook, bake and serve sets.

Action Appliance Sets — blenders, mixers, toasters.

The Ohio Art Co.

The Ohio Art Company has been making tea sets since
approximately 1920.

Ohio Art, party-planned tea sets include "protective polyme
coated lithoed metal and plastic."

Some of the sets are Story Time, Three Little Pigs,
Goldilocks, Red Riding Hood, and Humpty Dumpty. These
metal tea sets include three place settings.

Land of Oz comes with four metal plates and saucers, fou
plastic cups and goblets, plastic creamer, sugar, and flatware

Good Morning breakfast set includes the same pieces as Lan
of Oz plus a plastic fruit bowl and matching mechanical met;
and plastic toaster.

Sets are packed from two to six place settings.

THE **OHIO ART** COMPANY
BRYAN, OHIO 43506

The World of Toys

6-Worcester Toy Company
x 772
rcester, Massachusetts 01613

Worcester began making toy dish sets in approximately 1950.
ese sets are made of high-impact polystyrene with a wide
ge of patterns and designs and are packaged from two to six
ce settings.
Valt Disney character tea sets are one line. Other sets are
de to resemble pewter, woodenware, and ironstone.
Some of the pattern names in tea sets include Blue Dahlia,
sebud, Skandia, Denim Debbie and Dottie, Country Cousins,
ld Rose, Bouquet, and Columbia.
Play sets for the kitchen include Patioware Dinner Set,
chenware Set, and English China Dinner Set.
"Pop Art" mug sets have the Campbell Soup and Nestle's
ocolate labels and trademarks.

THE TEA-PARTY

POLLY, PUT THE KETTLE ON.

Coffee pot height, 3½ inches. Teapot height, 3 inches. Plate diameter, 2¾ inches.

Thomas Turner (1749-1809) became proprietor of the Caughley (or Salopian) Works, England, in 1772, after having served his apprenticeship to Robert Hancock at Worcester, England. In 1799 John Rose of Coalport purchased the factory.

This blue-and-white Oriental landscape design was made circa 1775-1790, with the "S" printed mark in underglaze blue. The set includes a water pot and cover, teapot and cover, creamer, sugar, four cups, and four saucers.

Sugar bowl top, 1¾ by 2½ inches. Sugar bowl height, 1-2/5 inches. Decorated in blue.

(blue)

Josiah Spode, Stoke-Upon-Trent, England, began as a potter in 1749. Ownership of the factory remained in the family until 1833 when it was purchased by Copeland who took Garrett as a partner until 1847. In 1847, Mr. Copeland's four sons joined the factory. The mark has had many changes over the years using the names Spode — Copeland — Garrett. The Spode company is noted for producing fine quality porcelain. This creamer and sugar was made by Spode — Copeland, circa 1875-1889.

Teapot height, 3½ inches. Saucer Diameter, 3 inches.

The English Staffordshire district made doll dishes, but these are not as plentiful as the dishes little girls used for their tea parties.

This set is decorated with blue and gold. The pieces included are a teapot and cover, creamer, covered sugar, four cups, and four saucers. This set was made circa 1900.

74

These sets all appear to have been made in Germany, circa 1890-1915.

Small tea sets or doll-sized dishes often were not marked. The cobalt blue color was popular in the late nineteenth century and early twentieth century and was used extensively by German makers.

Sets 1 and 2 appear to have been made from the same mold. The only marking on the bottom of the teapot and creamer are mold marks. The cobalt blue and flower set came as a six-place setting. Circa 1900. Teapot height, 4 inches. Plate diameter, 2¾ inches.

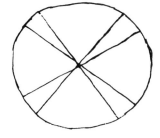

Set 3 was produced by Gebruder Heubach who also made dolls and novelty items. On the back of the pitcher is written, "A Present From Scarborough." Teapot height, 3¾ inches. Saucer diameter, 3 inches. Set of two — no plates.

Set 4 is a pretty, dark cobalt with portrait heads. Teapot height, 4½ inches. Saucer diameter, 3 inches. Two serving plates, 4¼ inches. Set of two — no plates.

Set 5 White with cobalt trim. Teapot height, 4½ inches. Saucer diameter, 2¾ inches. Set of four — no plates.

Set 6 White china with cobalt trim. Teapot height, 4¼ inches. Saucer diameter, 3 inches. Two serving plates, 4 inches. Set of two — no plates.

Set 7 Hand-painted windmill scenes. Teapot height, 5 inches. Plate diameter, 3 inches. Set of four.

Set 8 White with orange trim. Teapot height, 3¾ inches. Saucer diameter, 3 inches. Set of four — no plates.

In the nineteenth century, American dinner service sets were made with a variety of pieces. A number of these pieces can be found in children's sets.

Plates came in four sizes, the largest being dinner, then luncheon, salad, and bread and butter. Platters came in at least five sizes. Vegetable serving dishes, either covered or open were in round, oval, oblong, or square shapes. Soup tureens had a cutout in the lid for the soup ladle handle. Gravy boats had either separate or attached trays. There were odd-shaped service pieces to be used as relish dishes, bread trays, celery trays, large salad bowls, and butter dishes.

Sets also included individual service pieces. Cream soup bowls had two handles and were larger than coffee cups; whereas, soup bowls were wider in diameter and not as high as cream soup bowls. Sauce dishes for fruits or vegetables varied in size. Butter pats were about three inches in diameter. Bone dishes were about one-fourth the size of a dinner plate, and were kidney shaped. Small, open salts were about one and one-half inches in diameter. Cups came in a variety of sizes and shapes. There were coffee, cocoa, demitasse, and flared and squat teacups. Bouillon or consommé cups had two handles and were about the size of teacups.

Coffee, tea, or cocoa pots were sometimes made to match the dinner service set and may have had a matching serving tray.

European dinner sets were made separately from tea sets and did not include cups. By European custom after-dinner coffee was served in the drawing room.

This child's dinner service set has the impressed beehive or shield mark that could have been either Austrian or German.

The semiporcelain or soft-paste dishes were of finer quality than most play dishes. They were decorated in blue underglaze designs of children's pastimes, animals, and toys. The dress of the girl was an everyday type, quite plain, almost ankle length. The boy was wearing knickers and shirt with a wide, sailor-type collar or a loosely fitting blouse.

This twenty-piece dinner service set included: A covered bowl (4 inches high, 5¼ inches in diameter), an offset gravy or sauceboat with attached tray (7 inches), one platter (8 inches in length), large open serving bowl (6½ inches in diameter), medium-sized open serving bowl (5½ inches in diameter), small open serving bowl (4½ inches in diameter), one large serving plate (7 inches in diameter), six dinner plates (5½ inches in diameter), six smaller plates (5 inches in diameter).

This dinner service set was made by W. R. S. & Co. (William Ridgway, Son & Co.) Church Works, Hanley, England.

Charles Dickens established a weekly publication in April 1840, called *Master Humphrey's Clock.*

Master Humphrey was a character in Dickens' books, the writer of a serial consisting of different stories told to him by a group of friends. Humphrey's friends are characters from Dickens' earlier works such as Mr. Pickwick and the two Wellers.

No story of Humphrey's began until "The Clock" was wound. The clock was considered his beloved friend, his companion.

This set includes a soup tureen, covered vegetable dish, gravy pitcher, large platter (7 inches in length), two smaller platters (5 inches in length), two large plates (4 ½ inches in diameter), two smaller plates (4 inches in diameter), and two soup bowls.

The scenes are of children in the park, walking, sitting, and playing with a dog.

Pattern: Humphrey's Clock. Circa 1870.

Creamware is an ivory earthenware or semiporcelain that was first made by Wedgwood in the Staffordshire district of England. Wedgwood made a set of these dishes for Queen Charlotte, thus earning them the name "Queensware."

Since creamware was inexpensive compared to porcelain and lightweight to ship in the export market, it became popular and was copied by other potteries.

Creamware was usually quite plain, often with only an enameled color border. Sets were large and may have consisted of twelve plates, twelve soup bowls, five graded-size platters, and numerous serving pieces.

Black and green bands circa 1820. Plates and bowls, 3 inches in diameter. Platters range from 3 ¾ to 6 inches in length.

Around the 1850s, dinner service sets were made as toys, and some sets are still available. These sets are not usually marked. They are a semiporcelain, have quite a bit of crazing, some discoloration, and are hand-painted.

If you stack four plates and rub them back and forth, they have quite a low, almost hollow, sound.

This set is white with green and red hand-painted lines for decoration and either red or green trim on the handles.

Pieces included in this set are a tureen minus the cover (6 ½ inches in length), an open serving dish and two covered serving dishes (all 5 ¼ inches in length), one large platter (7 inches in length), one smaller platter (5 inches in length), three plates (4 ½ inches in diameter), four plates (4 inches in diameter), four plates (3 ½ inches in diameter).

Bishop & Stonier, Hanley, England were the makers of this dinner set. This Staffordshire pottery factory was in business from 1891 to 1936. The name of the individual pattern was often included from 1891 to 1910.

This charming blue-and-white set with a feathered edge is sometimes called Flow Blue.

This sets includes four small plates (2¼ inches in diameter) four larger plates (3¼ inches in diameter), four graded-size platters (4¼ inches to 5½ inches in length), soup tureen with ladle, sauce or gravy pitcher, and covered vegetable dish.

(blue)

PEMBROKE

BISTO ENGLAND

(brown)

HYDE

MILLAIS

These semiporcelain pieces were made by Ridgways, Bedford Works, Shelton, Hanley, England. This Staffordshire pottery mark was used from 1905 to 1920.

The platter (4¾ by 6 inches in length) and covered vegetable dish have a yellow flower design. The pattern name is Hyde. The complete set was sold, piecemeal, by a dealer in Freeport, the Bahamas.

The covered vegetable dish with the cobalt blue trim is the same size as the Hyde pattern. This pattern is called Millais.

This French soft-paste (faience) dinner set is an off-white or creamy color and is decorated with stencils in green and red. The design of the stencils shows a stylized type of flowers that were probably in vogue from about 1890 to 1930.

The large tureenlike covered dish, 5 inches high, does not have a cutout in the lid for the ladle. The next two covered dishes are made the same in a smaller scale, 3¾ inches high. Other serving pieces include a large salad bowl, a shallow bowl, a platter (6½ inches in length), and a large plate (5½ inches in diameter). The place settings include four dinner plates (4¾ inches in diameter), four saucers (3¼ inches in diameter), and three cups

This French soft-paste dinner set is very similar to the
[pre]ceding set.
[T]he handles are styled the same, but have a little change in the
[des]ign. Some of the pieces are shaped differently.
[T]he stencils are of blue cats with yellow flower designs on the
[bor]ders.
[T]he set has twenty-two pieces consisting of eight plates (5
[inc]hes in diameter), four cups, three saucers, gravy boat or sauce
[dis]h, pedestal dish, open bowl, covered bowl, and a larger
[cov]ered bowl.

Quimper, a town of many potteries located in France, is
[kn]own for its earthenware. This ware was decorated with the
[pea]sants' traditional costumes, their folklore, and farm animals.
[It] is often called Folk Art. It also came with a yellow
[ba]ckground with only flowers for decoration. They used bright,
[viv]id colors. Their work is a classic-type design that has been
[use]d for many years but is considered contemporary, today.
[Qu]imper is still being made for export.
[T]he H-B on the mark stands for two families, Hubaudiere and
[B]usquet of one factory. The word France was added after 1891.
[Th]is platter size is 4¼ by 6 inches.

(black)

The Blue Onion pattern is a familiar pattern that was designed
[by] Johann Haroldt about 1730 at the Meissen factory in
[Ge]rmany.
[J]ohann Haroldt introduced this pattern when underglazed
[blu]e was being developed. He used designs of Oriental patterns
[alo]ng with his designs of the Tree of Life, the chrysanthemum,
[th]e pomegranate, and a stylized peach (mistaken for an onion).
[W]ares made at the Meissen factory have the crossed swords
[ma]rk. The Blue Onion pattern was copied by other European
[fa]ctories.
[T]his set is a well crafted, hand-painted, underglazed blue
[po]rcelain circa 1880. Pieces included are a covered tureen with a
[pin]econe-type finial (4½ inches high), an open serving dish (4½
[inc]hes in diameter), a platter (5¾ inches in length), a serving
[pla]te (5½ inches in diameter), three plates, and three soup bowls
[(bo]th 4¾ inches in diameter).

Villeroy and Boch made this dinner service set at the Dresd[en] Germany, factory circa 1870s.

These pieces had been collected over a period of time and [are] in the same blue and white underglazed pattern as a coffee se[t in] the German section.

The dinner service includes twenty-eight pieces. They ar[e a] covered tureen (5¾ inches high), two platters (5½ inches [in] length), one large serving plate (5 inches in diameter), twe[lve] small plates, and seven soup bowls (4 inches in diameter), t[wo] small open dishes (2½ inches in diameter), and two gravy [or] sauce pitchers (3 inches high, 4 inches long).

A little girl could really serve just like mother with this German porcelain dinner set, circa 1870. Dinner sets genera[lly] did not come with cups.

This set is decorated with hand-painted cherries and inclu[des] six dinner plates (3½ inches in diameter), six soup bowls (3[½] inches in diameter), one soup tureen (3¾ inches high), two la[rge] platters (5½ inches in length), and ten more miscellaneous serving pieces.

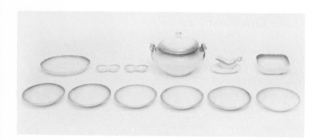

This German set with pink luster, was purchased as a set, [but] looking at the sizes of the pieces, one must ask, "Was this [a] stewpot with serving pieces, or has someone mixed pieces [here] through the years?" Luster on German dishes was popular in t[he] nineteenth century in both children's and adult's sets. This set [was] prior to 1870, but the texture looks and feels as if the set mig[ht] go back as far as 1830.

This set includes six bowls (4¼ inches in diameter), one [large] stewpot (5 inches high), plus five miscellaneous serving piec[es].

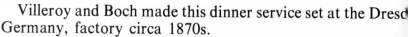

This German partial dinner service set, circa 1870, was nice[ly] made. Chickens, often used in decorating, form the center [of the] design. Each plate has a different transfer.

Pieces of this set include eight plates (3¼ inches in diamete[r], five smaller plates (2½ inches in diameter), one platter (4 inch[es] in length), and one serving bowl.

Small soup tureens may have been made with a set of play
ishes or produced as salesmen's samples.

A Limoges tureen has a royal-arms design with the words
"Grand Cafe Des Negociants" on the bowl. The top
was decorated as a leaf and has a nut-design finial; 5 by
3 ½ by 3 ¾ inches high.

DEPIERREFICHE
*
LIMOGES

B A very fine German white porcelain with blue bands
and trim. The fancy "H" on the bowl and cover would
mean it was made for a special family; 5 ¾ by 4 by 4
inches high.

C A white porcelain tureen with green bands and gold
trim has an Austrian designed border; 5 ½ by 3 ½ by 3
inches high.

D A white German porcelain tureen with gold bands was
made as part of a play dinner set; 5 ¼ by 4 by 3 ¾
inches high.

E This white pottery tureen with black sand flecks and
crooked finial was made as an inexpensive toy; 5 ¾ by
3 ¾ by 3 ¾ inches high.

F A tureen by Wedgwood, Etruria, England would have
been made as a child's piece circa 1890 in the Blue
Willow pattern; 4 ¼ by 3 by 3 inches high.

WEDGWOOD
ETRURIA ENGLAND

Top..

White and gold hand-painted by W. A. Pickard. 4 by 5 by 3 inches high, circa 1893.

Center..

Artist, E. Smith. 3½ by 5¼ by 2¾ inches high, circa 1893.

Bottom...

Decorated by Portrid J. Richardson. 3½ by 5¼ by 2¾ inches high, circa 1920.

Small Haviland tureens are often mistaken for children's pieces. A letter received from Haviland & Co. Inc., New York confirms "Haviland & Co. has never manufactured any miniatures."

In the book *Haviland-Limoges* by Serry Wood, published 1951, the small tureens are called sauce tureens.

In the book *Grandmother's Haviland* by Harriet Young, published in 1970, the small tureens are referred to as salesmen samples, to show style and pattern design.

The Haviland Company was founded by David Haviland 1842. He moved from New York to Limoges, France, for the purpose of establishing a factory to produce fine porcelain tableware for export to the United States.

Since that time the factory has retained the Haviland name. The mark has changed approximately twenty-seven times which makes it easier to date the pieces.

To Make Coffee

Take a good-sized cupful of ground coffee, and pour into a quart of boiling water, with the white of an egg and the crushed shell. Stir well together, adding a half-cupful of cold water to clear. Put into the coffee-boiler and boil for about a quarter of an hour; after standing for a little while to settle, pour into your coffee pot, which should be well scalded, and send to the table. The coffee should be stirred as it boils.

The two major differences between coffee- and teapots is the height of the coffeepot and the location of the spout.

The coffee grounds were added to the pot and allowed to settle, so, with the spout being located near the top, one would not get the grounds in the coffee cup.

From *The Everyday Cook-Book* (Published circa 1880)

illeroy and Boch began a new factory at Dresden, Germany 853. The china shown here is a white semiporcelain with blue erglazed pattern and was made at this factory in the 1870s. his style server with the high spout is considered a coffeepot. sugar bowl is 2 ½ inches high with raised lion's heads on the sides.

he pieces purchased with this set are: coffeepot with lid (6 es high), two creamers (2 ½ inches high), one sugar cover inches in diameter), four cups (1 ¾ inches high), three deep- saucers (4 ½ inches in diameter).

illeroy and Boch also made this coffee set at the Dresden ory using the same molds as the preceding set.

he decorations are done in underglazed blue. On one side of server is a girl with angel wings holding a small tree, and on other side is a boy carrying a shovel and a pail. The other orations are small objects such as toys (ball, top, and pull or items found around the house (salt box, coffee grinder, nel, spoon, scissors, needle, thread, books, horn, and violin). his set includes a coffee server and lid (6 inches high), mer (2 ½ inches high), covered sugar with a raised lion head ach side (2 ¾ inches high), four cups (1 ¾ inches high), four o-dish saucers (4 ½ inches in diameter).

Coffeepot height, 5¼ inches. Plate diameter, 5½ inches.
(Courtesy of Evelyne Helgesen)

(red)

Little elves decorate this porcelain coffee set that was made [in] Germany circa 1900.

The decorations include pink-to-yellow luster on the top edge[s] and cover in addition to the colorful elves. In one scene the elv[es] are holding pussy willows and are playing with a bunny rabbi[t.] In another they are pulling an old shoe.

The set included a coffeepot and lid, creamer, covered suga[r,] six plates, six cups and saucers.

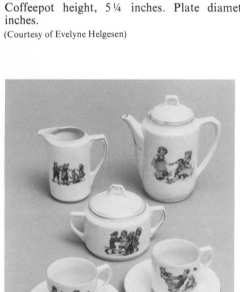

Coffeepot height, 5½ inches. Creamer height, 4½ inches. Sugar height, 3¼ inches. Saucer diameter, 4 inches.

Germany made some fine porcelain play dishes with detailed transfers and gold trim.

The transfer on the server shows two little girls with a dog an[d] toys. The creamer has two girls and two boys playing a gam[e;] the sugar has three girls and a boy holding hands in a circl[e] game; a cup shows two boys on a teeter-totter with two girl[s] watching; another cup has a boy and girl swinging around and [a] little girl sitting with her doll watching.

The children's clothes styles would date this set around 190[0.]

Coffeepot height, 6 inches. Plate diameter, 5½ inches.

(red)

This set was made by Beyer & Bock, Volkestedt-Rudolstad[t,] Germany. This is from the same mold as the Happifats set. Th[e] figures on this set have been called "Snowflake Elves" or "Creatures." The decorations include a blue band and very colorful figures.

From the shapes of this pot and cups, this service would b[e] called a coffee set. Pieces are a coffee server and lid, creame[r,] covered sugar, four plates, four cups and saucers.

Germany made this fine porcelain set with figures of children playing. The cartoon-type characters are playing active games such as football, baseball or roller-skating and are displayed in vivid colors on a white background. The mark includes only the country origin which would date the set about 1900, or a little later.

The server is shaped like a coffeepot with the spout being nearer the top of the tall pot. This service includes a coffeepot and cover, creamer, covered sugar, six plates, six cups and saucers.

(red)

Coffeepot height, 6¼ inches. Plate diameter, 5¼ inches.

Schumann & Schreider began a porcelain factory at Schwarzenhammer, Bavaria, in 1905.

This coffee service has character figures. One is a stubby man wearing a flat hat. He has wide-open eyes and a big fat nose and is smoking a cigar or a pipe. His companion is a penguin-like figure with an extra-long nose.

The set includes a server (6½ inches high including the ¾ inch fancy finial), creamer, covered sugar, six cups, and six saucers (4¼ inches in diameter).

1891

This German coffee set appears to be a child's set because of the small serving plates, the shapes of the cups, and the inferior quality.

The set is decorated with little birds and flowers. The 1891 impressed on the coffeepot, the 1892 on the creamer, and the 1893 on the sugar bowl are believed to mold marks.

Pieces included are a coffeepot, creamer, covered sugar, four plates, four cups and saucers.

Coffeepot height, 6½ inches. Plate diameter, 4¾ inches.

The following adult sets are included to help give you a comparison between children's play dishes and adult demitasse sets and to serve as an aid in both buying and selling.

Some of the features to help determine sets made for adults are:

1. Extremely fine porcelain that would not stand abuse.
2. Adult-type figures, such as the classical styles, or fine hand-painted designs.
3. Fancy elaborate finials and gold or silver trim.
4. The top diameters of the cups are usually over 2½ inches which is larger than most play dishes.
5. The height of an adult server is usually 6½ to 8 inches and a child's server is seldom over 6 inches tall.

(Courtesy of Le Trianon Antiques, Inc.)

The Berlin factory, Konigliche Porzellan Manufaktur, also known as KPM, was taken over in 1763 by Frederick the Great at which time the scepter mark came into use. Wares made at this factory may be referred to as "Royal Berlin."

This factory produced a porcelain comparable to Meissen and was noted for fine flower-painting and the beautiful designs of the services.

This set has the qualities of an adult individual service because of the fine porcelain, the miniature hand-painting, and the slightly larger cup.

The center designs were painted in puce color. The colorful border trim is glazed in yellow, red, black, green, and blue. The whole set is of exceptionally fine quality.

(blue)

This Von Schierholtz set looks as if it were made for adult demitasse service, or, as we may say, after-dinner coffee. It is a nicely made porcelain with hand-painted roses and molded rose finials on both the coffee server and the sugar bowl.

It is not a cocoa set because a cocoa spout would be a little higher and off the top rim, and a cocoa set does not include a creamer or sugar bowl.

The shape of the coffee server is like the 1870s Villeroy and Boch, but the whole set is on a larger scale.

This set includes a coffee server (7½ inches high), creamer (4 inches to the top of the handle), covered sugar (3½ inches high), six cups (2 inches high), six saucers (4¼ inches in diameter).

This white porcelain set was made by Johann Seltmann, [Ob]erpfalz, Germany, who began production in 1901. This [co]mpany made coffee and demitasse services plus gift items. This set is a finer quality than most children's play dishes. [Pi]eces included are a coffeepot, creamer, sugar, six plates, six [cu]ps and saucers.

Germany

(blue)

Coffeepot height, 7 inches. Plate diameter, 5 inches.

These two sets have a look of being adult demitasse sets. They [ar]e finely decorated and the cups are a little larger than those of [ch]ildren's sets.

The silver set has the words "Arboix, Colon, Sterling Silver." [Th]is is a porcelain with a sterling silver overlay. Silver left [ex]posed will develop a patina (dark iridescent tarnish) that can [be] a desirable quality.

The green set has a large tray (10 by 18 inches) for serving, [an]d the paintings are decorative pictures in the classical style. [Th]is, a fine porcelain with gold trim, was made in the porcelain [fa]ctory in Altrohlau, Bohemia, Czechoslovakia, which began [pr]oduction in 1883.

Arboix
Colon
Sterling-silver
27

(green)

Coffeepot height, 6 ¼ inches. Saucer diameter, 4 ½ inches. Set of six — no plates.

Victoria
Czechoslovakia
HF

(green)

Coffeepot height, 6 ½ inches. Saucer diameter, 4 inches. Set of six — no plates.

Spode is known for quality chinaware. (See Spode in doll dishes.) This set includes a teapot, coffeepot, water pitcher, creamer, sugar, and one cup and saucer.

Sometimes when seeing a set of dishes in smaller scale it i hard to determine if the set was intended to be a child's play s or if it is an individual service set.

This set appears to be an individual set because the teapot i bigger and wider than a play set's; also, the creamer and suga are a little large. This is a twentieth century mark.

(black)

Coffeepot height, 6 inches. Teapot height, 4¼ inches.
Pitcher height, 5 inches. Decorated in black.

Cocoa Sets

Chocolate

Take six tablespoons scraped chocolate, or three of chocolate and three of cocoa, dissolve in a quart of boiling water, boil hard fifteen minutes, add one quart of rich milk, let scald and serve hot; this is enough for six persons. Cocoa can also be made after this receipt. Some boil either cocoa or chocolate only one minute and then serve, while others make it the day before using, boiling it for one hour, and when cool skimming off the oil, and when wanted for use, heat it to the boiling point and add the milk. In this way it is equally good and much more wholesome. Cocoa is from the seed of the fruit of a small tropical tree. There are several forms in which it is sold, the most nutritious and convenient being chocolate, the next cocoa, then cocoa nibs, and last cocoa shells. The ground bean is simply cocoa; ground fine and mixed with sugar it is chocolate; the beans broken into bits are "nibs." The shells are the shells of the bean, usually removed before grinding. The beans are roasted like coffee, and ground between hot rollers.

From *The Everyday Cookbook* (Published circa 1880)

This cocoa pot was made in Germany, circa 1870. Cocoa pots are relatively close in size to coffeepots. The main difference is the design of the spout. The cocoa pot spout is very short and close to the top of the pot. The cocoa cups are taller than coffee- or teacups.

The only mark is a raised, star-type extra porcelain. These were added to give strength to the pot and will generally date before 1870.

Other shapes of porcelain used to add strength.

Cocoa pot, height 7¼ inches.

   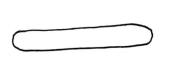

Glassware

Glass companies made pressed glass, child-sized table servic[e] sets (sugar, creamer, covered butter dish, spooner), water pitcher and glass sets, punch bowls and cups, berry sets, cak[e] plates, condiment sets, and castor sets, plus small versions o[f] other items that were made in adult sizes. These pieces are i[n] scale to playtime dishes and add realism to a table setting.

Most of the pressed glass children's pieces we find today wer[e] manufactured between 1870 and 1920. Some patterns are no[w] being reproduced in both clear and colors. The reproduced pieces are heavier than the old glass, and, in the colored glas[s] the shades are darker in the new pieces.

There were numerous glass companies during this period, some of which were in business only a short time. Ohio, Pennsylvania, and West Virginia were the main centers for gla[ss] companies because of the supply of coal and natural gas for fu[el] found in these areas.

Some of the glass companies that were known to make children's dishes were the U.S. Glass Co., Bryce Brothers Gla[ss] Co., Indiana Tumbler & Goblet Co., Cambridge Glass Co., O'Hara Glass Co., Bryce Higbee Glass Co., Heisey Glass Co[.] Ohio Flint Glass Co., McKee Glass Co., and Imperial Glass C[o.] Some companies made only one pattern and are not listed her[e.]

There are fine books written about pressed glass; therefor[e] this text will not go into more detail or pattern names.

ample of children's pressed glass

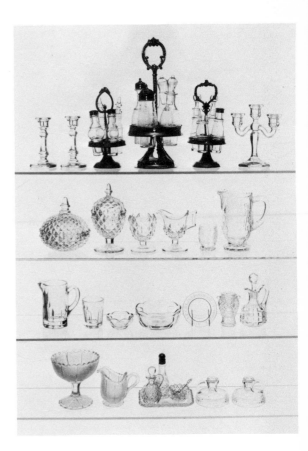

w 1 Two goblets (flattened diamond and sunburst)
  Punch bowl and cups (fancy, cut).

w 2 Small serving dish (star-type)
  Glass covered chicken
  Small round serving dish (cottage).

w 3 Unstemmed banana dish (star-type) (a calling card dish)
  Stemmed banana dish (fan-type)
  Round open serving dish (star-type).

w 4 Cake plate (fern)
  Cake or candy plate (thistle).

(Glass samples in rows 2, 3 and 4 may not have been designed as children's pieces.)

w 1 Candlesticks (round base)
  Castor set, 6¼ inches high (four sided)
  Castor set, 9½ inches high (American shield) (Patented May 22, 1877)
  Castor set, 6½ inches high (ribbon band)
  Candelabrum.

w 2 Table service set, covered butter, covered sugar, spooner, creamer (sawtooth), glass and pitcher (nursery rhyme).

w 3 Water pitcher and glass (flute)
  Individual and master berry bowls (flute)
  ABC ice cream plate
  Vase (daisy and button)
  Cruet (waffle).

w 4 Punch bowl and creamer (stippled band)
  Condiment set (English hobnail)
  Two low candlesticks (swirl).

Sears, Roebuck & Co., Chicago
Fall and Winter, 1927-1928

Also called pressed glass.
Pattern name, Oval Star.

Metal Tea Sets

Pewter, an alloy, is composed of approximately 91% tin, 7.
antimony, and 1.5% copper.

Pewterware was an important household item of commo
tableware used in Europe before china and porcelain. Pewt
was used in colonial America in such common items as plat
bowls, spoons, tankards, candlesticks, lamps, and coffeepot

Britannia is a silvery white alloy which contains 90% tin a
10% antimony. Another grade may contain 94% tin, 5%
antimony and 1% copper.

Pewter and Britannia articles can be hammered into shap
or worked into shapes by spinning or stamping. Casting methc
are used for handles, feet, knobs, and hinges.

Children's tea sets are usually referred to as Britannia. The
is a child's Britannia tea set in the Henry Ford Museum dat
1850-1860.

In 1902 the Sears, Roebuck catalog listed Britannia tea se
for less than one dollar.

Teapot height, 4 ½ inches. Saucer diameter, 2 ¼ inches.
Set of six — no plates.

Britannia Tea Sets.

No. 29R3
Britannia
set,consisti
of about
pieces, sil
finished te
pot, sug
bowl, sug
tongs, crea
er, plate
cups, etc. I
up in ne
pasteboa
box. Set..▶
Shipping weight, 7 ounces.
No. 29R393 Britannia tea set, consisting
about 23 pieces, silver finished. assortment same
above, but a little larger size. Per set............2
Shipping weight, 15 ounces.
No. 29R395 Britannia tea set, silver finishe
about 24 pieces, and still larger than above.
Price, per set....................... 4
Shipping weight, 28 ounces.
No. 29R397 Britannia tea set, consisting
about 24 pieces, silver finished dishes, very har
some filligree design and practical size, assortme
about same as above, and the largest size we car
Price, per set..7
Shipping weight, 40 ounces.

Teapot height, 3 ¼ inches. Saucer diameter, 2 ½ inches.
Set of six — no plates.

Enamelware is a metalware with a fused-on glaze. These
wares were manufactured in Germany, Yugoslavia, and
Czechoslovakia, besides in the United States. Many sets are
marked "Germany" and date from the 1800s.

Enamelware would have been used in the kitchen, much as w
use plastic, today, or it was purchased by families who could n
afford china.

These children's metal tea sets were made by The Ohio Art Co., Bryan, Ohio, which began making tea sets in approximately 1920 and continue to make tea sets and breakfast sets, today.

Other companies also made metal toy tea sets. Some sets are being made with all metal pieces, while other sets have some metal pieces (usually plates, saucers, and trays) and some plastic pieces (usually goblets, creamer, sugar, sherbets, and silverware). Cups are made in either metal or plastic.

Earlier sets often were decorated with Disney characters or nursery rhyme stories.

The mark on some of the earlier sets was "Ohio Art Co." written in very small script on the face of the plate.

Circa 1940
Teapot height, 2 ¼ inches. Saucer diameter, 2 ½ inches. Cake plate diameter, 4 ¼ inches.

Circa 1960
Saucer diameter, 4 ¼ inches. Plate diameter, 5 ¼ inches. Cake plate diameter, 6 ½ inches.

Sears Roebuck & Co., Chicago

Fall and Winter, 1927-1928

15-Pc. Unbreakable Blue Enamel Set
Made of metal, coated wtih rich turquoise blue enamel. Shaped teapot 4½ inches wide over all; 6 saucers, 2½ inches in diameter; 6 cups 1⅜ inches in diameter; sugar and creamer in proportion. Shipping weight. 1½ pounds.
49K1931 .... 98c

21-Pc. Cute Decorated White Enameled Set 98c
Attractive little metal set finished in white enamel trimmed in blue. Six 3½-inch plates; six 2¾-inch saucers; six 1¾-inch cups; shaped teapot, 3½x2 inches over all. Sugar and creamer in proportion. Shipping wt., 1¼ pounds.
49K1878 .... 98c

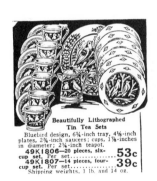

Beautifully Lithographed Tin Tea Sets
Bluebird design, 6¼-inch tray, 4⅛-inch plates, 2¾-inch saucers; cups, 1⅞-inches in diameter; 2¼-inch teapot.
49K1806—20 pieces, six-cup set. Per set 53c
49K1807—14 pieces, four-cup set. Per set 39c
Shipping weights, 1 lb. and 14 oz.

22-Piece Tea Set for Dolly's Party
Made of white pewter (not tin). Pitcher, 1⅛ inches high. Other parts in proportion. 4-inch metal tray. Shipping weight, 6 ounces.
69K7100 .... 19c

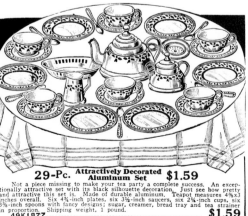

29-Pc. Attractively Decorated Aluminum Set $1.59
Not a piece missing to make your tea party a complete success. An exceptionally attractive set with its black silhouette decoration. Just see how pretty and attractive this set is. Made of durable aluminum. Teapot measures 4⅜x3 inches overall. Six 4¾-inch plates, six 3½-inch saucers, six 2¼-inch cups, six 3⅜-inch spoons with fancy designs; sugar, creamer, bread tray and tea strainer in proportion. Shipping weight, 1 pound.
49K1877 .... $1.59

To Meet Competition
19-Pc. Smaller Aluminum Set 79c
A pretty white metal finish aluminum set which will make sister's eyes pop. Shaped teapot, 4¼x2½ inches; four 4⅜-inch plates, four 3¼-inch saucers, four 2$\frac{5}{16}$-inch cups, four spoons, sugar and creamer in proportion. Shipping weight, ¾ pound.
49K1879 .... 79c

19-Pc. Our Leader Beautiful Satin Finish Aluminum Tea Set 98c
One of our outstanding values. You can't match it elsewhere at this price. We offer here the best value in satin finish aluminum tea sets we have been able to find. Fancy teapot, 4½x3 inches. Four 4¾-inch plates, four 3¼-inch saucers, four 2-inch cups, spoons, sugar and creamer in proportion. Shipping weight, 1 pound.
49K1873 .... 98c

Kitchen Items

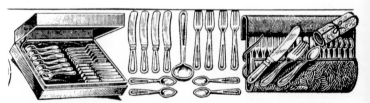

Knives
Forks
Spoons
Serving pieces

To set a table you would need "silverware." Most of what has been found is aluminum "Made in Germany," and often has "Like Mother's" stamped on the handle.

The sizes came in several scales, the knife ranging from about 3½ to 6 inches in length. The serving pieces were about 3 to 5 inches in length.

The United States also made "silverware" or tableware similar to the German sets.

The tableware which preceded aluminum was brass with porcelain handles, next was stamped metal with porcelain handles. These usually came in blue and white onion pattern and most likely came from Europe.

Another type of tableware was made of stamped metal which was then hand-filed. The hand-carved bone handles were held by two brass pins.

"Silverware"

Sears, Roebuck & Co., Chicago
Fall and Winter, 1927-1928

This complete German condiment and spice set consists of
[te]en pieces. The six large containers (3 ⅛ inches high) are for
[cof]fee, tea, flour, sugar, rice, and oatmeal. The six small
[con]tainers (2 ¼ inches high) are for cinnamon, nutmeg, allspice,
[clo]ves, ginger, and pepper. One medium-sized container for salt
[and] two cruets for vinegar and oil complete the set.

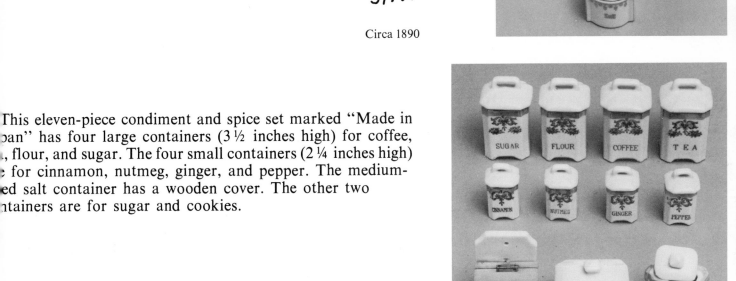

GERMANY

5772

Circa 1890

This eleven-piece condiment and spice set marked "Made in
[Ja]pan" has four large containers (3 ½ inches high) for coffee,
[tea], flour, and sugar. The four small containers (2 ¼ inches high)
[are] for cinnamon, nutmeg, ginger, and pepper. The medium-
[siz]ed salt container has a wooden cover. The other two
[con]tainers are for sugar and cookies.

Bread and canister sets were made in metal, and the sets that
[we]re available came in different designs and colors.
[The] Set at the top in picture has a decor of a Dutch boy and girl.
[He]ights of each piece are as follows:

[The] Set in lower half of picture is decorated with a gold stripe and
[go]ld lettering. This set is a little smaller scale. Heights of each
[pie]ce are as follows:

These sets were also made with a pattern of red strawberries
[an]d green leaves.

Cake and breadbox, 2¾ inches. Flour, 2¾ inches.
Sugar, 2½ inches. Coffee, 2¼ inches. Tea, 2 inches.

Breadbox, 2 inches. Cake cover, 1¾ inches. Flour, 2
inches. Sugar, 1¾ inches. Coffee, 1½ inches. Tea, 1¼
inches.

(Courtesy of Jane Moore and June Nelson)

Enamelware was made in many items for the kitchen. In th[e] Eastern United States this ware was called agateware or graniteware.

This gray and white spatter set includes twenty-three pieces: teapot with cover (4½ inches high), two cups, two saucers (inches in diameter), two soup bowls, one platter (4¼ inches length), double dish, mixing bowl or wash basin, fluted mol[d] frying pan, saucepan with a long handle, smaller pan with tw[o] small handles, colander, grater, funnel, dipper, pail, covered thunder jug, and a dustpan.

The dark blue enamel set consists of twelve pieces which ar[e] one small plate (2¼ inches in diameter), two larger plates (inches in diameter), one frying pan and one egg poacher (eac[h] 2½ inches in diameter), a spatula, a mold, a measure with handle (2 inches high), a saucepan, a small kettle, a dishpan wi[th] two handles, and a slop pail (2¼ inches high).

The darker blue utensil with a spout for pouring was made Yugoslavia.

Tan enameled bowl with green band and a hole for hangi[ng] was probably a washbasin that hung inside or outside the bac[k] door for washing before meals.

Mostly everything that was made for Mother's kitchen w[as] also made in a smaller scale for little girls to use for playing a[nd] learning. Cooking utensils came in a variety of materials a[nd] were well made.

This four-piece copper set includes a water boiler to be plac[ed] toward the back of the wood stove and has a spigot for hot wat[er] that really works. There are two large kettles and a saucep[an] with a long handle.

Water heater cover measures 6¼ by 3 inches. Cover diameters of the three kettles, 3½ inches. Large kettle height is 3¾ inches. Small kettle height is 3 inches. Saucepan height 2½ inches, with a handle 4¼ inches long.

Cast-iron frying pans came in many sizes and looked lik[e] Mother's in design. The waffle iron is also an exact copy in pl[ate] size. It is a "Stover Junior" made of cast iron with woode[n] handles and measures 3¾ inches in diameter. The base is 4 inches.

Heavy aluminum ware was made in the 1940s. The kettle a[nd] frying pan have an interchangeable cover.

Baking utensils also came in a variety of materials. Mixing bowls were a pottery with glaze on the inside or glazed all over. Glass bowls came in all sizes.

Utensils for mixing would most likely be made of aluminum or wood. Wooden rolling pins came in several sizes as did wooden butter molds. Small grinders were cast iron.

In 1924 the McKee Glass Co. made a "Betty Jane" nine-piece baking set, a "Betty Jane" six-piece glassbake juvenile set, a "Five-Piece Toy Pudding Set" and a "Five-Piece Toy Pastry Set."

Baking Utensils

Sears, Roebuck & Co., Chicago
Fall and Winter, 1927-1928

Every Little Cook Wants This!
8-Piece Pastry Set
Mother's outfit is too large to handle, but these are just right in size and really practical. Consists of one cup flour sifter, a real 5½-inch Betty Taplin egg beater, dough board 8x7⅝-in. rolling pin 10 inches long by 1⅜-inch diameter, 6¼-inch wood potato masher and three aluminum mixing spoons. Shipping weight, 1½ lbs.
69K9155 . . . . **59c**

Crocks were used for storage or pickling and were ususally kept cool in a cellar. Jugs were used for vinegar and cider and were stored in the cellar along with the canned goods that were preserved in glass canning jars. The small fruit jars pictured are 2¾ inches high, and the larger size are 3¾ inches high. The doll bottles "DOLL-E-TOYS by AMSCO" came in a wire rack so they could be set in a kettle of boiling water to sterilize the bottles.

Another interesting kitchen utensil set is this small, seven-piece German set, the largest piece is 2 inches high and is made in a pink luster porcelain.

Seven-piece utensil set (courtesy of June Nelson).

**Polished Aluminum
Sets—New Paneled Sides**
The pieces are large enough to use in practice cooking. New tube cake pan, 4½ inches in diameter. Others in proportion.
12-Piece Set for $1.29
Contains all the pieces illustrated. Shipping weight, 1½ pounds.
49K1864......................$1.29
6-Piece Special Set for 59c
Lipped saucepan, jelly cake pan, pie plate, mixing bowl, preserving kettle and frying pan. Shipping weight, 14 ounces.
49K1862......................59c

Sears, Roebuck & Co., Chicago

Fall and Winter, 1927-1928

Aluminum cook- and bakeware.

Aluminum pieces have changed the least in play dishes. Some of the baking pans in the 1927-1928 Sears, Roebuck & Co. catalog look the same as new pieces.

Some of the bakeware includes a measuring cup, mixing bowl, colander, gelatin molds, casserole dish, cookie cutters, cookie sheet, angel food cake pan, round and oblong cake pans, pie tins and muffin tins.

The aluminum cookware from the 1940s had red painted metal handles and red wooden knobs. Some of these pieces include a double boiler, a teakettle, and a roasting pan.

Before the days of buying and storing ice cream in home freezers, the only way to have some was to make it by hand using a machine such as the one shown.

This wooden tub was a style used in the early 1900s. White Mountain Junior was manufactured by the White Mountain Freezer Co., Nashua, New Hampshire. The wooden frame is 6¼ inches high and the top diameter is 5 inches.

There is a space between the center cylinder and the wood frame, this was for holding ice and rock salt which froze the ice cream as it was churned.

Colorful dresser sets have been made since about 1890. T[
continued to be popular into the 1930s.

Two such sets are shown: one from Germany on the left, a[
one from Japan (marked Nippon) on the right. Both contai[
hatpin holder, 2 inches high, a hair receiver, and a ring tr[

Cuspidors or spittoons were also part of the ladies' bedroo[
when snuff for the ladies was accepted. China cuspidors w[
common because they were so easy to keep clean, but they w[
made in all materials.

The cuspidor shown in the picture is made of brass and is 1[
inches high, 1 ½ inches wide.

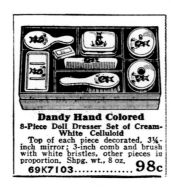

Dandy Hand Colored
8-Piece Doll Dresser Set of Cream-
White Celluloid
Top of each piece decorated, 3¼-
inch mirror; 3-inch comb and brush
with white bristles, other pieces in
proportion. Shpg. wt., 8 oz.
69K7103 .... 98c

Sears, Roebuck & Co., Chica[
Fall and Winter, 1927-1928.

Dresser Sets

Toilet sets came into fashion in the early 1800s. Washstan[
with a cutout for the basin became part of the bedroom
furnishings.

The earlier sets were made of pottery. Later, depending on [
means of the buyer, they were available in choices ranging fr[
plain white ironstone to elegant porcelain.

As the bowls and pitchers were made in larger scale, oth[
pieces were added. Some of these pieces were a soap dish,
sponge dish, toothbrush dish or mug, drinking glass or mu[
small pitcher for hot water, slop pail, and covered chamber p[

All of these pieces were also made in children's play size. T[
ad was published in the 1902 Sears, Roebuck & Co. catal[

OUR NEWPORT TOILET SET AT $3.75.

OUR NEWPORT TOILET SET is one of the very latest and handsomest
patterns put on the market, beautifully
decorated with yellow and pink chrysanthemum blossoms and foliage as
shown in the illustration, in addition to which every piece is heavily decorated with gold. The gold decorations are not simply lines and tracings as
are usually put on toilet sets, but a heavy deep stippled effect which gives the
toilet set a most luxurious appearance. We consider this set one of the handsomest we have ever been able to furnish, and being made by one of the most
reliable potteries in America, we can guarantee it to be strictly high grade.

Each set is carefully packed complete in a barrel to insure safe delivery
and shipped direct from the pottery in Western West Virginia.
No. 2R402 10-Piece Toilet Set, consisting of wash bowl, pitcher, covered
chamber (2 pieces), covered soap dish (3 pieces), hot water pitcher, brush vase
and mug.
Our special price...$3.75
No. 2R404 12-Piece Toilet Set, same assortment as the 10-piece toilet
set No. 2R402, with a large slop jar and cover added, as illustrated.
Our special price...$5.45

108

Pitcher height (handle), 2 ¾ inches. Bowl diameter, 3 ½ inches.
(Courtesy of June Nelson)

Pitcher height, 5 ½ inches. Bowl diameter, 6 inches.

Shapes

Tea   Coffee   Cocoa

These three German pots give a good idea of the shapes of pots used for serving tea, coffee, or cocoa.

The teapot is short, with the spout being near the bottom. T coffeepot is much taller, with the spout being nearer the cen or top of the pot. The cocoa pot is relatively close to the coffeepot in size, but the spout is molded at the top of the p

SHAPES

Teapot and tea

Coffeepots an

Chocolate or cocoa pot and

Here are some of the usual drinks from different countries, often served with meals, as listed by the Encyclopaedia Britannica.

Austria — coffee, or chocolate topped with sweetened whipped cream.

China — Jasmine tea served in small handleless cups.

England — tea with milk.

France — coffee, chocolate, or strong coffee diluted with half milk.

Germany — light beer, or medium roast coffee.

Greece — sweet black tea, and Turkish coffee.

Italy — dark roast coffee.

India — tea, or coffee.

Japan — tea.

Mexico — chocolate flavored with cinnamon.

Netherlands — tea, or coffee with cream.

Poland — black coffee or China tea.

Russia — China tea with cherry or strawberry jam.

United States — tea or coffee.

Kewpies — Happy Fats
Buster Brown - St. Nicholas
Sunbonnet Babies - Alice In Wonderland
Kate Greenaway - Brownies

Dinner Service Set by Wm. Ridgway Son & Co.
            pattern - Humphrey's clock
Glassware - Fernland table service set
            2 small open serving dishes
            Flat sided castor set - covered chicken
Flatwear - Brass with porcelain handles,
            Onion Pattern - made in Austria
Vase - Mosher - 4½ inches tall
Hutch - 43 inches tall, dishes top to bottom
            German procelain blue onion pattern
            German - white with pink luster trim
            English - blue & white, Bishop & Stonier
            Small German with many serving pieces
            Three blue and
            white English pieces
            Rocking Chair and
            two German
            Steiff Teddy Bears

Books - "The Brownies
            Their Book" &
            "Under The
            Window"

Melissa Krei and Mercedes Henderson
American Dinner service set by Cook Pottery Co.
Glasswear - Tulip & Honeycomb
Tablewear - German aluminum "Like Mothers"
Castor Set - American Shield 9½ inches high

Doll on the left - German Kestner 22 inches tall
Doll on the right - French Jumeau 23 inches tall
Table Service - English Salopian circa 1780's
Cookie Plate - German cobalt portrait plate

German Simon & Halbig Doll 22 inches tall
Ice cream table and chairs
"White Mountain" ice cream maker
Glass ice cream platter and ABC ice cream plates
Glasses by Federal Glass Co.
Spoons - German Aluminum

Melissa Krei is sitting in a caned Lincoln rocker
Oak Buffet 43 inches high with an individual tea set
    (Royal Berlin), brass candlesticks and a
    Seth Thomas mantle clock
China Cupboard 52 inches high - dishes top to bottom
    from England, Germany, Russia, Germany,
    Switzerland, Japan.

Mercedes Henderson is in a kitchen scene making
   waffles
The yellow cupboard is 36 inches high and filled with
   kitchen items.

French Steiner doll 15 inches tall
Dresser 19 inches high with a Nippon dresser set,
  hand mirror, and button hook.

Wash stand 17 inches tall
Pitcher 6 inches to the top of the handle
Bowl diameter 6 inches

English wax doll 16 inches tall, in her original
underclothes

Bibliography

Barber, Edwin Atlee. *Marks of American Potters*, New York
J & J Pub., 1976.

Danckert, Ludwig. *Handbuch des Europaischen Porzellans*,
Munchen, Germany: Prestel Verlag, 1974.

de Angelis, Marguerite. *Book of Nursery and Mother Goose
Rhymes*, Garden City, N.Y.: Doubleday & Co., Inc., 1954

Encyclopaedia Britannica, Chicago: William Benton, 1965.

Florence, Gene. *Depression Glass*, Paducah, Kentucky:
Collectors Books, 1974.

Godden, Geoffrey A. *Encyclopaedia of British Pottery and
Porcelain Marks*, New York: Crown Publishers, Inc., 1964

Godden, Geoffrey A. *Jewitt's Ceramic Art of Great Britain
1800-1900*, Rev. ed., London: Barrie & Jenkins, Ltd., 1972

Hartung, Marion T. and Hinshaw, Ione E. *Patterns and
Pinafores Pressed Glass Toy Dishes*, Des Moines, Iowa:
Wallace-Homestead Book Co., 1971.

Jackson, Mary L. *If Dishes Could Talk*, Des Moines, Iowa:
Wallace-Homestead Book Co., 1971.

McClinton, Katherine Morrison. *Antiques of American
Childhood*, New York: Bramhall House, 1970.

McClinton, Katherine Morrison. *Antiques in Miniature*,
New York: Chas. Scribner's Sons, 1970.

Papapanu, Sophia C. *Akro Agate Children's Line and Price
Guide*, Syracuse, N.Y.: Eastbrook Printing Co., 1973.

Penkala, Maria. *European Porcelain*, Rutland, Vt.: Charles E
Tuttle Co., 1968.

Ray, Marcia. *Collectible Ceramics*, New York: Crown
Publishers, Inc., 1974.

Ruggles, Rowena Godding. *The One Rose.*   1964.

Stout, Sandra McPhee. *The Complete Book of McKee Glass*
Kansas City, Mo.: Trojan Press, Inc., 1972.

Weatherman, Hazel Marie. *Colored Glassware of the
Despression Era*, vols. I and II, Springfield, Ill.:
Weatherman, 1970.

About The Author

Lorraine Punchard was born and raised in rural Wisconsin. She now resides in the Upper Midwest with her husband and three teen-age children.

Lorraine's interest in children's dishes began in her childhood when she received a cupboard of them from a neighbor who, herself, had played with them as a child. Of this collection, only the glassware remains. The pattern is Tuplip and Honeycomb and is shown in the color section with the two little girls.

Her interest in children's dishes has continued throughout the years and she has endeavored to collect all types of wares in this field. This book is a culmination of five years of research and study on the subject.